What reviewers say about this book:

"If you are an animal lover or of an adventuresome bent, you will enjoy reading Rosana Hart's *Llamas for Love and Money* She gives you humor, reality, resources, and some wonderful photos."
　　　　　—KLCC (Eugene, Oregon, National Public Radio)

"Packed with practical advice on all aspects of llama care, the easy, no-nonsense style of this book makes for compulsive reading... I was delighted to find a chapter on alpacas in this book and to read some very positive comments on these cousins of the llama."
　　　　　—*Camelid Capers* (England)

"Rosana Hart is quite well known to the world of llama owners and she is an accomplished writer... She always gives the reader the thoughtful side, the considered view... Well worth reading!"
　　　　　—*Llamas Magazine*

Also by Rosana Hart:
   Living with Llamas: Tales from Juniper Ridge

Thundercloud relaxed with Nelson Leonard after doing their banking. The local newspaper reported that the llama did not make any deposits uninsurable by the FDIC.

Llamas
For Love and Money

By
Rosana Hart

Juniper Ridge Press
Olympia, Washington

Llamas for Love and Money, by Rosana Hart
ISBN 0-916289-19-2

Published by: Juniper Ridge Press
PO Box 1278
Olympia, WA 98507-1278
(206) 705-1328; order line (800) 869-7342
Printed in the United States of America.

Second edition 1994

DISCLAIMER OF LIABILITY— READ THIS!!

The author and Juniper Ridge Press shall have neither liability nor responsibility to any person or entity with respect to any loss or damage caused or alleged to be caused directly or indirectly by the information contained in this book. While the book is as accurate as the author can make it, there may be errors, omissions, and inaccuracies.

Cataloging-in-Publication Data
Hart, Rosana
     Llamas for love and money / by Rosana Hart. -- 2nd ed.
        p.   cm.
     Includes bibliographical references and index.
     ISBN 0-916289-19-2 : $14.95
     1. Llamas. I. Title.
SF401.L6H37 1994
636.2' 96--dc20

Contents

About the Author

Rosana Hart began breeding llamas in 1982. She has also been a reference librarian, hypnotherapist, and workshop leader. She has a B.A. in Anthropology from Stanford University and a M.L.S. (Master's of Library Science) from the University of California, Berkeley.

With a mother who wrote engineering textbooks and a father who wrote science fiction (Cordwainer Smith), Rosana has been writing all her life. She wrote *Living with Llamas* and founded Juniper Ridge Press to publish it in 1984. She later edited and published Stanlynn Daugherty's *Packing with Llamas*. Rosana assisted her husband, Kelly Hart, on most of the half-dozen llama videotapes he has produced for Juniper Ridge Press. She is a member of the International Llama Association, which in 1991 awarded her a Pushmi-Pullyu Award for llama education. She is currently working on a walking guide to Olympia, Washington.

The author with Thundercloud

Acknowledgements

They say that people will talk more freely about sex than about money. The only sex lives I asked about were the llamas', but many llama owners freely discussed llamas and money, or just llamas, with me.

Special thanks to Linda Rodgers, Nelson Leonard, and Cathy Spalding for their review of this edition, and to Nard and Dennis Mullan for their review of the alpacas chapter. My husband Kelly has helped me in innumerable ways.

The following people have been interviewed for this book and/or commented on all or part of the original manuscript: Averill Abbott, Sharon Ableidinger, Carroll Albert, Heather Bamford, Larry Bannier, Bill Barnett, Fred Bauer, Stephen Biggs, Helen Bodington, Nancy Calhoun, Lou Centrella, Cecile Champagne, Ed Chlarson, Sylvia Coward, Stanlynn Daugherty, Danny and Katie Emrich, Chuck and Joanne Forest, Richard and Pamela Freeman, Coral Gibson, Bobra Goldsmith, Francie Greth-Peto, Reta Hamel, Erma Hast, Sheron Herriges-Smith, Marcella Hoeltzel, Carol Holland, Lake and Lawrence Hunter, Lynn Hyder, Peter Illyn, Paul Janes, Susan Jones Ley, Don Jorgensen, Neil Josselyn, Tom Landis, Toni Landis, Nelson Leonard, Dan Lospalluto, Bob Mallicoat, Frank McCubbins, Marty McGee, R. E. McMaster, Jr, Jack and Dee Meyer, Dan and Marilyn Milton, Sandy Mubarak, Bob and Marty Niccolls, Kay Patterson, George Peoples, Terry Price, Jay Rais, Jane Robertson-Boudreaux, Linda Rodgers, Steve Rolfing, Ken Rose, Ken Safley, Laura Sawyer, Daniel Schoenthal, Jamie Sharp, Russ Shields, Cathy Spalding, Tom Stammer, Marybeth Surrarrer, Susan Torrey, Charlene Trent-Lewis, Ralph Uber, Cutler Umbach, and Beula Williams. There were also several people who preferred not to be named, and I may have forgotten somebody. Thanks to all.

My appreciation also to the many other llama owners who have enriched my understanding over the years, either in person or in print. Special gratitude goes to *Llamas* and *Llama Life*, as well as to Drs. LaRue W. Johnson, Murray E. Fowler, and the other researchers whose work is improving the lives of llamas.

Llamas are superb teachers of being present in the moment. It is one of their many gifts to us. Thank you, llamas!

CHAPTER ONE:

Llamas!

WE GOT our llamas for love and money.

There's been lots of love. The joy of hiking in the mountains with inquisitive llamas as trail companions, the thrill of watching a newborn llama wobble to its feet, the fascination of observing the interactions of llamas with each other—these and many other pleasures have been ours. We've developed friendships with other llama owners from all around North America, and we've developed very close bonds with llamas. There has been an abundance of love, filling (and sometimes breaking) our hearts. Llamas for love? You bet!

Our llama breeding has been profitable, but the process has called for lots of patience, and it's been a steeper learning curve than I expected. We learned patience when our first llama babies were all males, worth a fraction of what the females sell for, and when one of our three female llamas proved difficult to get pregnant. But eventually fortune smiled on us. Llamas for money? A qualified yes: many llama breeders make money but not necessarily as much or as quickly as they expected. Commercial llama packing and other llama-related activities also offer income opportunities.

Why are llamas popular?

All across America, people are taking on the joys and challenges of raising an animal whose beauty is legendary and whose intelligence is such that the Indians of South America call the llama their 'speechless brother.'

Llamas have appeared on television magazine shows and in publications such as the *Wall Street Journal*. It has been reported that

Divinity and Matthew Ableidinger share a quiet moment.

Michael Jackson, Johnny Cash, and other celebrities own llamas. Kim Novak owns a whole herd.

Why is all this happening? Just what are llamas, and what are they good for?

Llamas are woolly, intelligent pack animals native to the high Andes mountains that run down the middle of South America. Sometimes called 'ships of the Andes' for their central role in transporting goods for the great Inca empire, llamas have been domesticated for six thousand years or more. Besides packing, the Indians used llamas for wool, in religious ceremonies, and as sources of food. Llama dung—small pellets, rather like those of deer—provides fuel. There are still millions of llamas in the Andes, owned by Indians and still used in many of the traditional ways, although their use as packers has been supplanted in many places by motorized vehicles, mules, and horses.

In recent years, North Americans in increasing numbers have fallen in love with these animals. From zoos and the exotic animal world, llamas have moved onto the ranches and farms of America. Most prevalent initially in the West, llamas are increasing in popularity in the Midwest, on the East Coast, and throughout Canada.

Llamas are used and enjoyed in several ways: as pack animals, for pleasure, for showing, for their wool, and for breeding.

Llamas are a natural for people who enjoy outdoor recreation. Hikers are discovering how gentle, tractable, and easily trained these animals are. The llamas can carry the packs and also provide companionship. Some enterprising llama lovers have made a success of offering commercial llama pack trips.

Animal lovers often admit, "I've always wanted a llama!" With an innate dignity and serene yet inquisitive approach to life, llamas are a joy to be around. Many people who are not hikers derive great pleasure from just being with their animals, watching the antics of the babies, the posturing of the males, and the herd interactions. (If you have always wanted a llama, I suggest that you now start wanting two; they are such social animals that a solitary llama is apt to be lonely.)

One llama breeder, Marty Niccolls, expressed a widespread feeling about llamas. "The first time we saw them," she told me, "it was a kind of meeting of minds. Some animals you might feel superior to, but I look at the llamas and I say, 'Okay, you understand what I'm doing and I understand what you're doing.' "

While llamas vary greatly in personality, they generally enjoy people. They completely lack the slavish devotion of dogs. There is typically a more cat-like aloofness in a llama. You can go on vacation without worrying that your llamas will pine for you.

Sometimes people are disappointed to find that the average llama doesn't immediately want to be cuddled and petted. But when you take them on their own terms, they are a continuing delight to watch and to be with. Some llamas I call *bridge llamas* as they have personalities that bridge the gap between llama and human more than most of their species. These animals enjoy very deep connections with people.

Some people now use llamas in therapy, often with children. The llama's role in stress reduction is famous world-wide: my uncle once sent me a clipping from a Singapore newspaper, describing how llamas help North Americans to relax. It's true!

People enjoy taking llamas in parades and to other public events. Well-mannered llamas have been to many shopping malls, nursing homes, and schools. People are teaching their llamas to drive to cart. Llama shows and fun days are becoming more common, whether at county or state fairs, under the auspices of llama organizations, or put on by individual llama fanciers. Both halter classes, in which the llamas are judged on their appearance, and performance classes, which show llama-human teamwork in action, are popular.

Llamas produce a very nice wool. While relatively few llama owners are themselves spinners, many people do comb or shear their animals. They may have the wool made into garments and rugs for their own use, or they may sell the wool to shops or to people who visit their ranches. Llama wool varies considerably in quality. The amount, color, and kind of wool on a llama is an important factor in the price of that animal, but it's more for aesthetics than for the utility of the wool in producing yarn.

Breeding is the main source of income from llamas and it's also a thrilling aspects of llama ownership. Once we'd had one birth, I was hooked. I wanted more babies, the sooner the better! I was to discover that birthing can be an emotional roller coaster.

Danny Emrich, a llama owner who has worked at large llama ranches for years, comments, "To me, llamas represent something real. They eat grass. They poop on the ground. They have babies. You can do things with them. They provide some of the things that we need as people: clothing, food. They represent a lifestyle. They keep me close to the land. Llamas add such an incredible dimension to living."

Some history

Zoos have been homes to llamas in this country for over a hundred years, typically breeding with their offspring generation after generation. Beginning in the late 1920s, William Randolph Hearst imported some llamas to roam the hills of his grand San Simeon Estate on California's central coast. He had a dozen llamas in 1931. Around that time, the United States government banned importation from any country where Foot and Mouth Disease was present. Since the ban, some animals have come in from countries free of the disease, or in more recent years by undergoing quarantine processes.

It has sometimes been said that the basis of North American stock was only the Hearst herd, but in actuality there were also the zoo animals and some others. Still, it is true that thousands of North American animals are descended from a small number. It has been estimated that at the time of the importation ban in 1930, there were two hundred fifty llamas in this country. Many of those were actually guanacos, an undomesticated close relative of the llama, or llama-guanaco crosses. After Hearst died, Roland Lindemann purchased the San Simeon llamas, which numbered between thirty and forty animals. He took them to his Catskill Game Farm in Catskill, New York, where llamas are still bred today. Lindemann also purchased some llamas from zoos. This Catskill herd grew over time, and was one of several sources from which Dick and Kay Patterson selected llamas for a herd which has numbered over five hundred animals. Many breeders today own some Patterson llamas or descendants of Patterson animals.

During the 1980s, a number of llamas and alpacas were imported from South America. Many breeders welcomed the new blood lines. while others were initially reserved. Today, many llamas are described as "part Bolivian" or "part Chilean" offspring of these imports. All told, there are probably somewhere around 50,000 llamas in North America now. That's very small compared to the over fifty million dogs, forty million cats, or ten million horses. There are over a quarter of a million donkeys and mules, counted together.

Alpacas

Alpacas are smaller than llamas, bred by the Indians for their wool where the llamas were bred more for packing. Alpacas have a somewhat more herd-oriented disposition. Until recently, there were very few alpacas in the United States, mostly in zoos. But during the 1980s, several hundred were imported and now there is a thriving business. In North America as in South America, the alpaca industry

Alpacas are smaller and woollier than llamas. Here,
a llama is sitting and two alpacas are standing.

is focussed on the production of outstanding wool.

Alpacas and llamas share a North American ancestor, which
was also precursor to the camel. About three million years ago, some
of these animals went over the Bering Sea straits when there was a
land bridge, and became the modern day Bactrian and Dromedary
camels. Others moved into South America. Some of their descendants
became the guanaco and the vicuna, wild animals which still exist
today. Archaeological evidence suggests that the llama was
domesticated from the guanaco, and the alpaca from the vicuna. The
four species are known collectively as *lamas*.

This book is primarily about llamas, but Chapter Seven is
about alpacas, and there are occasional mentions of them elsewhere.

Making money with llamas and alpacas

Combine animals which are beautiful, useful, and fascinating, with the
possibility of making a profit, and it's obvious why so many people

are looking into owning llamas and alpacas.

For many years, demand for llamas grew faster than the available animals, and prices went up and up. In the 1970s a breeding pair of llamas sold for around $1500. Prices gradually rose, and then in the early 1980s, there was a plateau, with most females selling for $4,000 and most males for $500. By 1987, females generally began around $7,000, and males around $500 or $750, but prices for both sexes had spread out, with prices for the most desirable animals climbing much higher. By 1990, the starting figure for females was closer to $10,000. The fanciest show animals commanded prices in excess of $100,000. The rise in prices was at times rather frenzied, and around the time of the Persian Gulf war and the recession, prices began to decline. Today, they are under half what they were in 1990. What will they do in the future? All the factors that make llamas so wonderful are still there, plus it's a more mature industry. I expect to see a wide range of prices, reflecting various uses and preferences. (There is more discussion of prices in chapters 5 and 10.)

The difference in base prices between the sexes is because only one male can breed numerous females, as many as thirty or forty. Males not likely to be used for breeding still begin around $500 to $750. Stud potential males begin at a few thousand dollars.

At present, there are only a few thousand alpacas in the United States, and these animals sell for considerably more than typical llamas. Many of the people who own alpacas are llama owners. There are the beginnings of llama and alpaca industries in New Zealand, Australia, and Europe.

This book

This book will introduce you to the business of llamas in North America today: caring for the animals, breeding and birthing, buying and selling, promoting and showing. One chapter describes alpacas. I describe commercial llama packing and a variety of other activities. I discuss the income potential of llamas and the future of llamas.

A final chapter, the Resource Guide, provides you with access to further information about llamas and alpacas. It lists organizations to join, magazines to subscribe to, and books and videotapes to look at—all complete with names, addresses, prices, and descriptive comments.

The facts and opinions in this book are derived from three sources: interviews with a wide variety of llama and alpaca owners; a review of what's been written on llamas in North America; and my own experience and perspective as a llama breeder and owner for ten years.

I talked with dozens of llama and alpaca owners from around the United States and Canada in researching the material in this book. Interviews were conducted by telephone, at conferences, and on ranches. I focussed my attention on the many owners of small to medium sized herds somewhat more than on the major breeders, because small breeders' experience is more directly pertinent to most readers of this book. Over and over, I was impressed with the great joy people feel at living with llamas, their enthusiasm for the future, and their ability to balance all this with thoughtful appraisal of the possible pitfalls which individual llama owners and the industry face.

Since raising llamas is a relatively new business, there is not a great deal in print. The literature I drew upon came from conference presentations as well as from articles in two extremely useful llama periodicals. *Llamas* began in 1979 as a three-page information-sharing newsletter and has progressed to a full color magazine of a hundred pages or more, published eight times a year. *Llama Life* is a quarterly publication with many thought-provoking articles. Both periodicals cover alpacas to a lesser degree. I have also drawn upon articles in the other publications listed in the Resource Guide; because this is not a scholarly work, I haven't footnoted my sources.

My perspective

My husband and I bought our first llamas in 1982, so we have seen the llama community grow and the industry mature. We never owned more than thirteen animals at a time. In 1981, Kelly and I bought undeveloped acres in the rugged and snowy Oregon mountains, near the town of Ashland, and got to work making it our home. Soon we bought our first llamas, two males. We were so enchanted with them that we added some females. I wrote about these llamas in my first book, *Living with Llamas,* which we published in 1984.

After that, we continued to breed llamas, had a day-hikes packing business on our ranch for three summers, and expanded our publishing efforts. This is the third book we've published, and Kelly

Like people, llamas vary in personality. Thundercloud greets a ranch visitor, but Posey is more timid.

has put his film background to work in producing six videotapes on lamas and several on other topics. In 1988, we boarded our llamas with good friends (themselves llama breeders), sold our mountain ranch, and moved into Ashland. We missed the daily interaction with llamas, but we liked having the time to concentrate on books and videotapes. I noticed, too, that after having lived with llamas for so long, they had become a part of my awareness in a subtle yet permanent way. We found ourselves so caught up in our activities that we rarely went out to visit the llamas.

In 1992, we made another major shift, moving to Olympia, Washington, and selling our herd to the friends who had been caring for them so ably. Now we are publishing books and videos on a wide range of topics and enjoying, at least for now, an urban life. For the first time in a decade, we don't own llamas. I rather thought I always would, but life brings changes!

I am not a llama expert; many llama owners know as much or more than I do about llamas. All my life I have been a lover of information and books. I used to be a librarian in a public library system in California, and I enjoyed exploring together with someone else the resources that would tell them what they wanted to know. The same impulse motivates this book. I write about llamas to share what I and others have learned, to make it easier for newcomers.

This is a personal book, filled with stories. Another llama owner writing a book about the business of llamas would tell different stories—or no stories—and perhaps come to some different conclusions. I have tried to represent the breadth of the llama industry by doing many interviews, but ultimately everything on these pages has been filtered through my own awareness. I encourage you to talk to a variety of llama owners and to read, especially the magazines.

My sense of the future of llamas in North America is optimistic. There are so many people who would love to own llamas, and there are so many ranches and rural homes that already have the facilities. I expect to see llamas become a common domestic animal.

As llamas bring joy and pleasure into our lives, they help us to see that people are not the only sensitive, intelligent beings. We may know this from dogs, cats, or horses, but because of their nature and their newness on the North American scene, llamas are particularly able to break through our established patterns of thought and thus to renew our perspectives.

CHAPTER TWO:

Llama Care

IN ORDER TO KEEP LLAMAS, you will need fenced land, with a shed or barn. People who don't have land can board llamas out. You may have to make preparations to compensate for extremes of climate. The llamas will need feed, water, health care, and training. You'll need to transport them. There will be some record-keeping, and you may want insurance. You should know a little about llama personalities, and there are some considerations of human personality as well. This chapter will discuss these topics.

Land

People thinking of buying llamas often live on rural or semi-rural land. They may have been trying to find something to do on it, perhaps something which doesn't take too much time. They may like the idea of raising animals but may not want to raise a creature destined for the dinner table.

Llamas do well on many kinds of land and in many climates. There isn't a precise rule for how many llamas can be kept on how much land; it really depends on the situation. Llamas have certainly been kept in fields of an acre or less. The pertinent factors include grazing, exercise, visibility, your convenience, the need to separate animals, and llamas' need for companionship.

Llamas will graze on grasses and browse on shrubs and trees. If you just have a few trees in a pasture, you will sooner or later need to wrap wire mesh around them, to keep the llamas from killing them by eating the bark off. Llamas have a powerful instinct to wander around tasting this and that. The more they can do so, the happier they are. If they might overgraze your land, consider rotating the animals through more than one field.

The larger the area available to your animals, the more they will be apt to run around and get some exercise. Studs may get more exercise in less space than females and babies, because many studs spend a lot of time walking the fence line nearest the females. The babies love to run, especially around dusk—we call it the "Indianapolis Five Hundred"—and get up considerable speed if they have room. For overweight llamas, room and incentive to run is particularly important.

In thinking about the lay of the land, consider how visible the llamas will be to your house. Some people will care more about this than others. To me, one of the greatest joys of living with my llamas was waking up in the morning and looking out the bedroom window at the animals. Often one or more of the ladies would be sitting just under the window, keeping an eye out for when we might get up and feed them. It was comforting to be able to see the llamas at night too. Once in a while, one of the llamas would make the alarm call at night. We had floodlights we could flip on from the house, so we could quickly scan the fields, usually saving ourselves a trip out into the wind or snow.

It would be prudent to give some thought to the security of your herd. Attacks by domestic dogs are a greater risk than theft. We kept a Komondor livestock guardian dog on our ranch. She alerted us to anyone driving in as well as to any dogs within barking range. The things that made her such a good protector for our llamas were also sometimes difficult. She was extremely dominant toward all other dogs, and she could quite happily bark for hours at night. I think she regularly conversed with a dog whose distant barks we could barely hear. Getting a dog from one of the several breeds of livestock guardian dogs is a step that calls for research beforehand and attention afterwards. There have been some tragic problems with guard dogs and llamas.

You can design the layout of your ranch with security as one of the factors, including such simple things as gate placement. Some owners tattoo International Lama Registry ID numbers in llamas' ears, which can make it possible to recover a stolen animal. Microchips are also used.

Many breeders like to keep very pregnant females near the

house, where it's easy to check on them. Especially in extreme climates, layout should be designed with convenience of care in mind.

If you have male and female llamas, the land will need to be divided into more than one fenced area. Males and females are generally kept apart except for breeding. You might have an animal who needs to be isolated for medical reasons, or a new llama you're quarantining apart from the herd for a couple of weeks or more. At birth it is sometimes necessary to separate the mother and baby from other females.

If you choose to wean babies rather than letting the mother do it, you will need separate spaces for mothers and babies. Forced weaning can be heart-wrenching, and seems to go best if the mothers and babies can't see or hear each other, though this isn't always possible. Many breeders are now letting the mothers wean naturally, usually around eight months. (Not all mothers will do this, so you may have to intervene.)

If you are buying a couple of males, you may do fine with just one pasture. Groups of males in the same pasture will fight at times; ours would chase each other around for about twenty minutes a day. It was good exercise for them and they didn't hurt each other. You do have to judge the personalities of the animals; certain of our males just didn't get along with each other, and we kept them apart. Some active studs may not be able to share a pasture with any other llama. Llamas are very herd-oriented, and an animal that must be alone in a pasture should at least be able to see other llamas.

However many fields you have, there does seem to be a principle that you sometimes need one more! Some separations can be created temporarily, with movable stock panels or portable electric fencing.

If your land is hilly, or if you can create a hill, the llamas will enjoy it. They love to go to the tops of hills.

Plants poisonous to llamas might exist on your land. This is not always easy to figure out; one good place to start is with your county extension agent. The problem plants will vary with the locality. There have been some llama fatalities from poisonous plants. Llamas do not have an instinct to avoid North American poisonous plants.

Boarding

If you want to have llamas but don't have suitable land, the possibility exists of boarding your llamas. You might rent pasture nearby, and take care of the llamas every day yourself. It's probably more common to keep your llamas at the ranch of another llama owner, who provides care.

If you just want one llama for packing, boarding it out is a way to meet its needs for llama companionship. It's also rather common for people who own two geldings for packing to board them someplace, usually at a lower price than if the boarding included the intricacies of caring for females.

Prices and the details of arrangements vary greatly. The lowest I've ever heard was a dollar a day. I've also heard one hundred dollars a month.

Who trains, who pays for feed, who calls the vet, what responsibility the person boarding the llama has for breeding difficult females, or in case of illness or accident: all these should be clearly agreed upon.

You needn't even keep your llamas nearby; in some situations, the owners and the herds are hundreds of miles apart. Clearly, this is more of an investment situation than a family pet. Another common situation is for parents and adult children to buy llamas together and keep them in one place.

When we decided to sell our ranch and move into town, we boarded our llamas with some friends, Linda Rodgers and Nelson Leonard of Elk Hill Farms in Eagle Point, Oregon, not far from where we lived. This worked out well for several years. Linda and Nelson gave our llamas devoted and skilled care, in many ways better than we ever provided! When we were discussing how to do the finances, we came up with a straightforward agreement: they would do all the day-to-day herd management (care, training, showing animals for sale), and we would make the major decisions, such as who to breed to whom, who to sell and for how much, with their advice. They would not be financially responsible for any loss, injury, theft, or death of our animals, nor would we be financially responsible for any actions related to the boarding of our llamas. We could each use the studs that the other ones owned at the time.

As for payment, we paid a boarding fee of so much per day per animal; the amount changed a time or two. Included in this fee was the cost of all feed, including all nutritional supplements. We paid the feed bills within a month of their submitting them to us, but the remainder of the boarding fee wasn't due until an animal was sold. (Even then, the maximum amount due was limited to whatever we received for the animal minus what we estimated we would have to pay in income taxes. So if we sold a llama for $5000, and estimated the taxes were going to run us around $1500, what we owed naturally depended on our outstanding bill, but in no case would exceed $3500. Otherwise, we could have had a negative cash flow from selling an animal.) Some of the boarding fee could be taken in llamas, and they had the right of first refusal on all llamas we offered for sale.

We paid veterinary bills, other incidentals, and mileage when they hauled our llamas. After they stayed up around the clock with a sick newborn, we added an hourly rate for extraordinary labors.

While llama prices were high, our arrangement worked fine. But when we were moving away and trying to decide what to do about our llamas, we regretfully concluded that paying significant boarding fees could preclude making a profit. Since we would be too far away to really feel much connection with the animals, we were greatly relieved when Linda and Nelson offered to buy our herd. We do have visiting rights!

A couple who breed llamas told me that they keep a few llamas for a friend who lives in another state. The friend pays for feed and vet bills. When the breeders sells a baby llama from the friend's herd, they send half the income to the friend; the other half is their compensation.

Averill Abbott has boarded her llamas with another llama owner, Sally Wegner. "When I first did it, I couldn't afford to pay a whole lot of money, but I was willing to give them more money if I made more money," Averill told me. "If one of my animals had a baby, I would give ten percent of the sales price of that animal. We agreed on a bottom boarding price in any case. If I decided to keep a baby female, then we had a set price. At the time, it was six thousand dollars for a female, so I would owe Sally six hundred dollars. That worked out well. I paid when I sold an animal."

Fencing

Llamas are rather easy on fencing, and various kinds are used. Many llama owners use wire mesh fencing, New Zealand smooth wire fencing, or wooden rails. Barbed wire is not necessary or recommended for llamas.

"No-climb" wire mesh is an excellent choice for fencing. Posey is well protected from the dog.

I like to see higher fencing, five or even six feet, because you're fencing out dogs even more than fencing llamas in. If dogs—neighbors' or your own—could possibly be a problem, put in a very good fencing system.

Probably the best fencing is the "no-climb" fencing. That's a wire mesh two inches by four inches, which can be attached to any kind of rail fencing. Mesh fences with larger openings can be dangerous, as the llamas can become entangled in the mesh. This did happen to one of our llamas once, and necessitated a vet visit and stitches to the leg he had accidentally stuck through the fence.

New Zealand fencing, a group of smooth wires applied under tension, has been popular, partly because it can easily be electrified. In fact, it needs to be electrified to be sure of keeping dogs out. If the electricity fails, your protection is less. The llamas quickly learn to leave the fence alone. Unfortunately, there has been at least one death, where a valuable llama was rolling, became lodged under an electrified bottom wire, and died from the continuous electricity. In another incident, a llama owner noticed one of her animals under the hot wire and was able to turn the power off in time. Considering the potential problems if the power is off or if it's on, I'm not much of a fan of electric fencing.

The stories of dogs attacking llamas are rather numerous. It isn't only young llamas who have suffered bites, though they are most often the ones fatally injured. Coyotes are less often a problem than dogs. Good fences will greatly decrease the chances of such a tragedy.

Llama breeder Larry Bannier of Tennessee was very thorough. "My perimeter fence is six-foot chain link, and since there are a lot of dogs in my area, at the bottom of my chain link fence I put out three-foot hog wire. It's laying down flat on the ground around the entire perimeter on the outside. I take this crimper and I take these hog rings and I clip the fence on the ground to the bottom of my chain link fence. And then I lay logs over it so any dog that's on the perimeter can't dig under because he's standing on the fence. I've laid fallen branches all over the fence. Dogs are not smart enough to go back three feet to start digging."

No matter how good your fence, if the gate opens, the llamas are likely to go adventuring in the big, wide world. And when they've had their fun, there's a reasonable chance they'll return home. Sylvia and Roy Coward own two adult males they bought from us, Poco and Tumbleweed. Sylvia wrote to us that while she was feeding them, the gate accidentally opened. "The llamas took off down the hill to our neighbors' place, where they stood on their hind legs and swore at each other, just outside the bedroom window. Then they headed west. We got in the truck with some gear and drove down river. We came back, and Roy thought he saw one at the top of the hill. I hiked up there, but it was only a branch of a tree. A passing driver said the llamas were two miles down the road and heading east at breakneck speed. They'd never been in that area before. I called the highway patrol. They had already been notified. We drove three miles down and back, and never saw them.

"A neighbor called, and said he chased them off the road, and they were headed up Black Mountain. So I had a mental picture of coyotes, wild cats, and never seeing them again! Then about an hour later a caller said they were on another road. Then another said they were at the bridge. Roy had gone a few minutes earlier. I jumped in the truck and took off.

"I met them half way down the hill—they were coming home. I was able to halter Poco, and I tied him to a power pole. He lay down. Tumbleweed wouldn't let me catch him. My sore feet decided to walk Poco back up the hill. Tumbleweed followed. I called and kept walking, and he followed us down to the corral. We all walked right in the gate. Whew!"

Shelter

Llamas need a shelter, to get out of the rain, snow, wind, and sun. It needn't be fancy. Three-sided is usually fine, with the open side not facing the direction of the wind. They will also do well in a barn, though some owners have observed that llamas aren't fond of dark interiors in the daytime. Especially if you are designing facilities for a good-sized herd, plan your shelter and your fencing for convenience and speed of routine chores. For example, it's handy to be able to move the herd from one place to another, selecting out certain animals. Visibility and flexibility of function are desirable.

An unlikely danger, but one that you can guard against, is that spontaneous combustion sometimes occurs in bales of hay. Consider this in designing your hay storage, and be sure to put any extra-heavy bales away from barns. Barns that have more than one exit that the llamas are used to are safer.

A chute or very small stall is extremely useful for veterinary care and your own routine work. There are some portable ones that can be bought, but large, strong llamas have dragged some of them; be sure that couldn't happen with whatever you install. Or you can build one yourself. We got along without a chute at first, but once

Llamas need a shelter, to get out of the weather.

Kelly built one, we used it constantly. I highly recommend you start with one. Also extremely useful is a ten by ten catch pen, particularly for use with the very popular TTEAM approach to training and handling llamas.

Climate

Llamas are being raised in all North American climates, from Alaska to Florida. They take cold weather quite well; as llama researcher Dr. Murray E. Fowler has pointed out, llamas and alpacas are better designed for withstanding cold than heat. Nevertheless, llamas are being raised in the extremely hot climates of the southern United States. The owners make sure their animals have ways to cool off, including plastic wading pools and in some cases air conditioning. Birthing is usually scheduled for more temperate parts of the year.

Adequate shade and water are, of course, essential in the heat, and careful daily observation is called for. Shearing has become an important part of heat management programs in recent years. Some wool, often about three inches, is left on the animal, to insulate from heat and protect from sunburn. When woolly studs are shorn (usually after numerous photographs have been taken of them with their long tresses), frequently their sperm count has improved during the summer months.

The llama periodicals often run articles recounting how owners have coped with hot weather. Even so, some animals have been lost because of heat. Not all problems occur in the hottest climates; serious problems have even been reported from the Pacific Northwest on summer days with temperatures in the eighties. This is unusual, though.

Feed and water

Llamas do very nicely on a diet of grass hay, fresh water, and a vitamin-mineral supplement.

While some people have plentiful pasture, many llama owners also feed hay, at least for part of the year. It is possible to keep llamas on land that is marginal for other livestock, as the llamas are very efficient at extracting nourishment from the plants they eat and they need less protein than many other animals. Our ranch, in the mountains of Oregon, was on steep, rugged land. I enjoyed the feeling of using land that wasn't suitable for most farming uses.

Few llamas in this country are in danger of being underfed, but many are overfed. Start with large flakes of overly rich alfalfa hay, throw in generous handfuls of grain for treats, and you've probably got a fat llama. Llamas can get fat even on grass hay. One well-known llama researcher, Dr. LaRue W. Johnson, is always urging llama owners to get their fat llamas into condition, by limiting their feed and by exercising them. He thinks that the problem arises because people don't realize how very efficient at using their food the llamas are. Evidently in South America, where the forage is not that abundant, llamas do put on weight during the rainy season, which they then lose in the dry season.

Some breeders find that letting the mothers wean the young llamas, which seems to happen around eight months of age, instead of performing the more customary human-intervention weaning around five or six months, can be helpful in keeping the weight off a mother who is prone to gaining. (Not all mothers will wean their babies themselves, so you may still have to intervene. A mother whose prior babies have been human-weaned, or one who has recently lost a baby, may be less apt to wean on her own.)

A vitamin-mineral supplement should include selenium if it's needed in your area. Selenium is a necessary trace mineral, but it can be toxic if too much is ingested, a potential problem in some parts of North America. Simply by asking ranchers, veterinarians, or the local agricultural extension service, you can find out the status of selenium where you live and where your hay comes from. Different breeders supplement with different things: loose mineral salts, salt blocks, and/or special formulations for llamas. Nutritional research on llamas is reported at conferences and in the llama periodicals.

Llamas need a lot less water than other livestock. They generally drink a few gallons a day, with working animals and lactating mothers requiring more than other llamas. The water should be clean and the vessels frequently cleaned out. In very cold weather, if electricity is available, many people welcome a heater to keep the water from freezing on top. Such heaters can be dangerous; they need to be grounded properly and installed with an eye to safety.

Health care

Llamas tend to be quite healthy animals. Routine health care may include annual vaccinations for tetanus, clostridial diseases, and in some areas, rabies and leptospirosis. (Some llama owners have learned from their veterinarians how to give their own vaccinations, thus saving on veterinary costs and having a needed skill in case of emergencies. You really have to know what you are doing, though.)

Llamas are subject to intestinal parasites, so you need to take a sample of their stools to your veterinarian two or more times a year. If worms are present, there are several medications which effectively treat them.

Llamas are usually very stoic about pain or illness: they may not show any signs unless a problem becomes quite advanced. If you suspect a problem, do watch the animal closely and don't postpone calling the vet.

At our ranch, with a herd size averaging eight to ten, we have averaged one or two health problems per year. They have ranged from things as simple as removing porcupine quills to greater difficulties, including the heartbreaking death of a favorite llama. Overall, I don't think the list has been at all bad for the number of animals and years.

You may find yourself working with your veterinarian in emotionally trying situations. If you can, find a vet who is interested in keeping up with the literature on llamas, whom you personally get along well with, and who isn't so busy that it will typically be many hours before you can get help. It's worth spending some time going around and talking to different veterinarians and llama owners in your region. Also have the name of a back-up vet—also skilled in llama care—for those inevitable times when yours is unavailable.

Veterinarians can learn about llamas from the textbook by Dr. Murray E. Fowler listed in the Resource Guide; a number of llama owners have given it to their vets, or at least given them the ordering information. There are workshops for veterinarians, sometimes held in conjunction with the annual conferences of the llama associations. Also, veterinarians often phone others who are experienced with llamas to discuss a case. The International Llama Association (ILA) lists a veterinary Hot Line in its membership directory, for precisely this purpose. Many of the numbers are answered all day and night, and all are for veterinarians only.

For your own learning about llama health care, I highly recommend that you buy a book, *Caring for Llamas: A Health and Management Guide*, by Claire Hoffman, a veterinarian, and Ingrid Asmus, long a ranch manager for Bobra Goldsmith's large Colorado herd. (Publication details are in Chapter 12, the resource guide.) It includes a lot of detailed information.

Male llamas must have their sharp fighting teeth removed. These teeth are in the sides of their mouths, coming in when the llamas are between two and three years of age. A veterinarian can anesthetize the animal and do surgery, or the teeth can be cut off at gum level using veterinary OB wire. This latter method may sound gruesome, but llamas must not have the same kind of nerves in their teeth as we do. Many people have observed that the llamas tend to become calmer as the process goes on; that is, once they have had one or two teeth cut off, they are more relaxed about letting you finish the job. (I noticed this once, doing our high-strung Whiskers' teeth.) If it were hurting them significantly, I would expect an opposite reaction. How to do this is demonstrated at llama conferences. It is important to remove these teeth on any male or gelding who may be pastured with other llamas or who may be used for breeding. If the sawing method is used, sometimes it must be redone the following year.

Another part of routine llama care is cutting their toenails. Not all llamas need this done. If those who do need it live on rocky

*Like people, llamas do have their arguments now
and then. For this reason, llama owners remove
the males' fighting teeth.*

ground, they may need it less frequently than if their pasture is soft. Cutting toenails is much easier if the llama has learned to accept handling of its feet. Nail trimming is also demonstrated at conferences and written up in articles.

If you live in an area which has white-tailed deer, and that's much of the Midwest and East, there can be a dangerous parasite called the meningeal worm. Llamas are also susceptible to liver flukes, parasites which live in marshy areas in various parts of the United States. These problems are not widespread, but if you're in a danger zone, knowledgeable local llama owners should be able to tell you about them.

Ticks and rattlesnakes can pose problems, at home or on the trail. I routinely pull several dozen ticks off our dogs every year, but have only seen one tick on a llama—and that tick wasn't biting. I have read a couple of reports of llamas having problems from ticks. The llama habit of gently blowing on items which arouse their curiosity has occasionally resulted in a rattlesnake bite on the nose. Call your veterinarian immediately if you suspect a snake bite; if you go packing in snake territory, learn what to carry to provide care.

The life span of the llama is often estimated at between fifteen and twenty-five years. The llama industry in this country is so new that there is still much to learn about these animals. Fortunately, there are dedicated and skilled researchers now involved with llamas.

Transporting llamas

Llamas can be transported in conventional stock trailers, trailers adapted from other uses, covered beds of pickups, and even in vans. It's important to ensure that the llama is unable to bump into the driver of the vehicle or to jump out. If the vehicle is almost but not quite adequate—for example, if you have an open pickup or a van with no divider—temporary barricades can be added to create this security. There should be proper ventilation and protection from the worst extremes of temperature.

Llamas travel with aplomb. They may eat a bit while travelling, but you don't need water sloshing around while the vehicle is moving. Just give the llamas a chance to drink at rest stops now and then. If you take some of their droppings with you in a little container, you can sprinkle them on the ground at rest stops. Because llamas like to go where a dung pile has been started, they often travel on very long trips without ever using the vehicle for a bathroom.

If you will be taking your llamas to schools and public appearances, to shows or pack trips, or if you will be doing a lot of buying and selling, then you will surely need something to transport the animals. If you don't expect to take them anywhere, then your only need might be an emergency trip to the veterinarian.

Many llamas are transported long distances across the country. Commercial livestock transporting companies can do this. Costs vary, but I've heard around a dollar a mile. To find out about these companies, ask breeders in your area. Some companies advertise in the llama periodicals and in the free *Llama Catalog*, published by the International Llama Association. Some of these companies specialize in llamas and alpacas only. Be sure any animals being transported are well insured while on the road. If you buy llamas at an auction, insurance and transportation can customarily be arranged there.

There is some paperwork involved in transporting llamas across state lines. Many states requires a health certificate, indicating that a veterinarian has recently examined the animal and found it to be healthy. It makes sense to be sure your animal is healthy when you

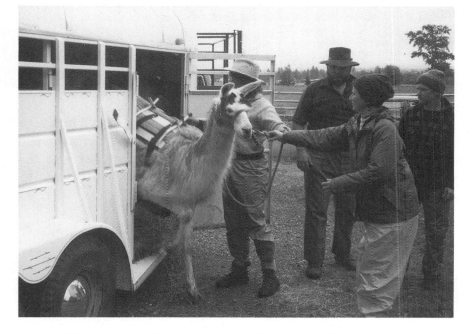

Llamas are often transported in conventional stock trailers.

will be travelling with it. Health certificates are required at auctions, shows, and other gatherings where llamas will be together. Some states also require special tests, such as for brucellosis, tuberculosis, anaplasmosis, and blue tongue. Some of these tests are rather controversial, with the allegation being made that they can produce false positives and negatives on llamas. Very few states actually have checkpoints at the state line. To find out what is needed for your state, contact your State Veterinarian. Your veterinarian or local public library can probably supply you with the correct phone number. At this writing, llamas from the United States cannot be transported into Canada, due to concerns the Canadian government has about livestock health.

Training

The intelligence of the llama, combined with its good memory, makes it an enjoyable animal to train. As noted llama trainer Bobra Goldsmith often points out, somewhere around the fourth time that you show a llama what you are asking of it, it catches on. And in many instances, that's all you have to do. The llama will remember. That's quite different from the number of times I've had to tell a dog to heel or sit before it would reliably do it!

Some things do take longer; for example, any llama may require several sessions before you can handle its feet, and one whose temperament is rather jumpy will likely require more.

One popular approach to llama training is T.T.E.A.M., or *Tellington-Jones Equine Awareness Method*, developed initially by Linda Tellington-Jones for horses and now used with many other animals. Marty McGee, a llama owner who has adapted the method for llamas, is well-known for her workshops on these techniques. Debra Potts in Oregon is also a qualified T.T.E.A.M. practitioner for llamas.

Information on a variety of training methods is available through books and videotapes. Betty and Paul Barkman, Jim Faiks, and Helen Bodington are other trainers who have contributed to our understanding of llamas; the Resource Guide lists many books and videos.

There are many llamas who are rarely handled, but every llama should be taught a few basic things: at least, becoming accustomed to being caught and haltered, leading, and loading into a vehicle. It's best if every female in your herd will stand quietly as you touch her abdomen and teats. The ability to milk her could save the life of a premature or weak baby who is unable to stand and nurse in the first few days. It's also exciting and reassuring to be able to feel the fetal movements in late pregnancy!

Not every llama owner has the time or the inclination to train llamas. In many parts of the country, you can find llama trainers. Some of them advertise in the national llama periodicals, while others are only known locally.

One thing I enjoy about training llamas or dogs is that many of the principles I come to understand better in working with the animals also hold true for people: the importance of timing in positive reinforcement, for example. My favorite training book, Karen Pryor's *Don't Shoot the Dog*, explores these principles.

Record keeping

Llama owners keep records in many different ways. You can write almost everything on a calendar, either a wall one or a notebook one. Some llama businesses sell forms designed specifically for llama record-keeping.

Our forms consisted of two pages per llama, reproduced here. I created a simple computer database, but tended not to get around to using it, so for me a system that was easy to pick up worked better. When our llamas moved over to Elk Hill Farms, Linda Rodgers used her own system. As she had been a nurse practitioner for many years, she gives each llama its own folder, and keeps its records with the most recent pages on top. She also makes use of Post-It notes for reminders of upcoming inoculations and so forth.

Other people offer computer programs, or you can create your own with any database program. Much as I love computers, I think that a computer program only makes sense for a medium to large herd, once remembering who is related to whom gets a little difficult. Then it would be quite nifty to be able to call up the genealogies of two animals and see if they are related, back a few generations. I've seen ads for computer programs in the llama magazines.

In any case, a notebook is always handy, and would also be a good place to keep photographs of all your animals. When you buy an animal, try to get photographs of its ancestry as far back as

INDIVIDUAL LLAMA RECORD

NAME:
SEX:
BIRTH DATE: BIRTH WEIGHT:
ILR NUMBER: OUR RANCH NUMBER:
HOW AND WHEN ACQUIRED, PRICE:

PHYSICAL DESCRIPTION, WITH DETAILS OF MARKINGS:

WHEN AND TO WHOM SOLD, PRICE:

REMARKS:

OFFSPRING:

The first page of a simple llama record system.
Parentage isn't included, as a registered llama
would have its ancestry on the registration form.

possible. When Blossom was born, she looked a great deal like her sire's mother, and we pored over the photos we had, comparing the black-and-white markings to the inch!

Registering llamas

The International Lama Registry has grown along with the llama and alpaca industries. Considering the modest costs and minimal work, I highly recommend registering your animals and purchasing registered animals. (If an animal you buy is not registered, you may not be able to register it or its offspring. The current address and phone of the ILR are in the Resource Guide; contact them with any questions.) The ILR encourages owners to tattoo the animal's ILR number in its ear

Llama # ____   Page ____

INDIVIDUAL LLAMA RECORD FOR _____

DATE   EVENT   COMMENTS

*A page like this can easily be used for notes on
training, health, etc.*

or use a microchip, but this is not required; photos may be submitted instead.

Another reason to register your animal is so there will not be confusion about names. Once you register a name, nobody else can register an animal with that identical name.

Llama insurance

Life insurance for llamas is available as *named perils*, listing specific perils and excluding illness, or *full mortality*, covering death from almost any cause. Naturally, the latter is much more expensive. Many llama owners, especially of large herds, carry no insurance, feeling that they have enough animals to self-insure. I asked a number of people if they carried insurance. Some did, but many said they hadn't gotten around to it. We carried named perils on our more valuable animals, and when we had a female llama whose purchase funds had come from a second mortgage, we carried full mortality on her for a while. It's not difficult to find llama insurance agents; they advertise in the magazines, send out mailings, and attend some llama events.

Llama personalities

There is as much variety in llama personality as there is in human. Genetic factors are at work here, but environment and training play a great part as well.

I've mentioned before that llamas are very herd-oriented. For that reason, many llama breeders will not sell a llama into a situation where it will be solitary. I certainly wouldn't. Their happiness depends in large measure on being with other llamas. Linda Rodgers commented that llamas are so communicative that for a llama to be alone would be like living in a country where nobody spoke English!

You should know about the 'berserk male syndrome.' This is a fairly rare problem, but potentially tragic. Essentially, if a male llama fails to distinguish between how he acts around other llamas and how he acts around people, he can be dangerous to the people. This is most commonly encountered in bottle-fed males, or in other males that have been handled a great deal when young, perhaps because of a health condition. They may lose their natural reserve toward people. This can be cute in a baby, but dangerous in an adult.

Llamas, like many other species, go through an imprinting

process when they are young. If a young llama is misimprinted due to extensive handling during its early impressionable period, it will be confused regarding its social interactions with other llamas and with people.

There is a wide spectrum of 'berserk' behavior: some males may occasionally knock somebody down, while others may try to attack everyone. In some cases, llamas have had to be put down.

There is still a lot for us to learn about this syndrome. In the meantime, most breeders don't handle their young males more than necessary. Many use a 'fake mother' if they have to bottle-feed; this is a device that somewhat resembles a llama. You put the bottle into it, and hopefully it keeps the baby from considering you as the food source. Still. if the bottle-fed or much-handled baby is male, gelding makes it less likely that problems will occur. There are a few well-respected breeders who have successfully trained intact bottle-fed males. But they have a lot of experience.

If you are a first-time buyer, I suggest that you don't buy that friendly little male that comes up to you in the pasture just like a puppy dog; better to chose a more aloof animal. Don't buy a bottle-fed male unless you discuss the whole situation thoroughly with some other llama breeders besides the seller. Stay away from llamas from petting zoos, because of their early, extensive interaction with humans.

Sometimes males who have been kept alone as adults develop behavior problems. "I've seen quite a number of males with odd personalities who were kept as singletons," Tom Landis told me. "It's easier to screw up a solitary llama than one that has company. I don't think all single llamas have problems, though."

Llama trainer Bobra Goldsmith has often been consulted about problem llamas. She says, "I am strongly against selling any young male to someone who does not have other llamas. I have been consulted by people who bought what we know were absolutely normally raised males—raised by their mothers and not petted or coddled—and kept them in a single-llama situation. Around eighteen months of age, some of those have jumped on their owners.

"The owners that care the most have had these problems. I think they tend to treat the llama more like the family dog, and therefore it starts to relate to humans like herd members. I think the eighteen-month-old llama who jumps on someone, and has no prior history of problems, is probably just doing it out of play. I think this can be corrected, and if it is corrected right away, I think the llama will not end up being a berserk animal."

A bottle-fed female may or may not be pushy, but she is less likely to be dangerous. The difference is in the nature of the sexual behavior of the animals. However, a friend of mine purchased an extremely dangerous female, who exhibited the worst of the berserk symptoms. "She attacked me viciously when I took away a cat she was watching," the breeder said. This llama was a bottle-fed one who didn't live with other llamas until after she was adult.

Human personalities

Llamas are being raised by people with all kinds of backgrounds and all kinds of personalities. But I see some common threads. Most llama owners are animal lovers, of course, but many have a real passion for working with and understanding llamas.

Llama owners may not start out any more patient than the average, but the process of breeding teaches you. When you have to wait almost a year to see the results of breeding two animals, which itself may have taken more months than you'd hoped, you have no choice but to wait.. Watching a female who was due to give birth last week is another time when you learn patience. Or how about being a few years into breeding llamas and not yet recovering the amount you've spent, let alone seeing a profit?

Stressful situations can arise: a sick llama when your vet's out of town, a difficult birth, a loose llama on a packing trip. It's worth thinking about how you handle stress. I don't always do well, and I had some difficult times. I knew this could happen when we got the llamas, but I figured the joys would be greater than the stresses. They were.

If you purchase llamas with your spouse or partner, your ability to make decisions together will get a good workout. What if one of you welcomes the inevitable visitors who just drop by to see the darling llamas, while the other one wants to put up a locked gate and NO TRESPASSING signs? What if the kids promised to help feed the llamas but don't want to when it's raining?

Many people find working together to be one of the benefits of being in this business. It's an added bonus of owning llamas: they will give you chances to grow personally in ways that seemingly have nothing to do with them.

CHAPTER THREE:

Breeding

LLAMA BREEDING BEGINS long before the day that you put a male and a female together. Breeders can spend months mulling over which stud to try with a female, and why.

As babies were born, we observed what the breedings produced. We saw temperament passed down from both parents, and saw the mother's influence as the baby grew up under her care. We saw conformation elements combine from the two parents, sometimes in surprising ways.

It's always fun to see the coloring. Whiskers, mostly black with a spot of white on his face, and Posey, mostly brown with white, black, and gray on her face in what is called 'original type' coloration, had three babies together: one mostly white with a little black, one mostly black with a little white, and one original type who was apricot-colored rather than the medium brown of Posey. There are principles of color inheritance, but predicting color is not simple. Sometimes I joked that we could be as likely to get a pink and green baby as anything else.

There is drama in the breeding encounter. How quickly will the female sit down for the male? How long will he breed, and how many times? How many days till she spits him off? One summer we weren't sure which of our females were open, so we took Levi on lead into the ladies' pasture. He approached Juliet, who immediately sat down. As they bred, Lil Bit came and sat down next to them, announcing that she wanted a turn too. The babies played around them all. Sex among llamas can be a sociable matter.

How it works

Llama reproduction is rather unusual. Rather than having an obvious heat cycle, the female ovulates after she has been bred. The mating process triggers her hormones; the technical term is *copulation-induced ovulation*. Rabbits, cats, mink, and some other animals are also induced ovulators. This makes it handy for breeding at times of your choosing, in accordance with the climate and other scheduling needs you might have.

In a few herds, people let a stud run with the females. This doesn't give an exact due date, but it does increase the chances your females will be bred immediately if they should lose a pregnancy without your knowing it.

It's far more common for people to hand-breed: put a male and female together, observe the breeding, and then separate the animals. This is repeated the next day or the day after, often for several days, typically until the female spits off the male. The dates are put on a

Sex among llamas can be a sociable matter.

calendar. Hand-breeding is a good term for it; sometimes you're out there in the pasture with the animals, pulling aside the female's tail, observing the males' position, or otherwise trying to help the process.

If her tail is rather woolly, it's typically trimmed a bit with scissors or tied temporarily with vet-wrap. When breeding, the male's penis turns clockwise, and if it encounters wool before it finds the female's vaginal opening, it can get badly tangled up in the wool, and lacerated—even to the point of infertility. So trimming both the males' and the females' wool in the genital areas is an important and increasingly common precaution.

If you take the female to the male's pasture, he will be more at home and less apt to be intimidated by the female than if you took him to her pasture, especially if she has a dominant personality. Some breeders prefer to take both the male and the female to a relatively small pen, so that the initial chase will not be so extended. If you do this, the male will very soon know what the pen is for; he probably will be as assertive as he would be in his own field. And of course, if he lives with other males, you couldn't put the female in with the crowd.

Once the animals have bred, how do you know the female is pregnant? You can test for pregnancy by field-testing: putting the female and male together again, after perhaps three weeks have gone by, to see if she will sit down for him. Over time you get to know your animals, and what their behavior means. If the stud is very aggressive or the female very submissive, she may be more apt to sit even if she's pregnant. Another variation is just to bring the male and female together across a fence, and to observe the female's actions. If her ears go back and she threatens to spit, or does spit, it's likely her hormones are doing something. This can be done with just one person, where it can require two or more if you are trying to remove a spitting female from the pen of an amorous male.

"Once you know your animals well, field-testing can prove invaluable," Carroll Albert commented. "We do a lot of progesterone checking, but we've yet to prove our mature llamas incorrect in their assessment of pregnancy status!"

You can send blood samples to a lab, about twenty-one days after breeding. Some breeders learn to draw blood themselves; others have their vet do it. The progesterone level is an indicator of pregnancy. But it's not fool-proof: a female can give progesterone level readings which would suggest pregnancy, yet not be, if she has a retained corpus luteum. This isn't common, but it certainly can be frustrating. Since many female llamas don't look very pregnant even at the very end of their terms, you can be thinking the baby is due any day when there is actually no baby. Conversely and also rarely, some females can have a very low progesterone count and still be pregnant.

Two ways to avoid these situations are for a veterinarian to do a rectal palpation for pregnancy, or to use ultrasound. If your vet has the expensive equipment, ultrasound is a good way of testing. Ultrasound can be used rectally, which—like rectal palpation—can be somewhat traumatic for the llama. Now becoming more popular is transabdominal ultrasound, where the equipment is placed on the outside of the abdomen. It requires more expertise on the part of the veterinarian. All of these procedures are best done within a restraining chute or small catch-pen.

Many breeders test again around sixty days, and perhaps again later, as it's not uncommon for a pregnancy to end spontaneously. One ranch, High Llama, tests at 21, 45, 120, and 210 days.

At present, artificial insemination, embryo transfers, and genetic engineering are not major factors in llama breeding. These topics are controversial. The three main llama associations, the International Llama Association (ILA), the Llama Association of North America (LANA), and the Rocky Mountain Lama Association (RMLA), have all suggested that the International Lama Registry not register offspring resulting from AI and ET, contending that these techniques would exacerbate the already existing problems of a small gene pool and the changing look of llamas. But not all breeders agree with this position.

Another technological breakthrough is more widely appreciated. In the past few years, blood typing tests have become available. The Serology Lab of the School of Veterinary Medicine, University of California, Davis, reports that it has used blood typing to rule out possible sires in 85% of the cases where a female was bred to more than one stud. Many breeders are having their herds, or at least key animals, blood-typed. Males who have produced ten or more offspring are now required by the International Lama Registry to be bloodtyped. DNA fingerprinting has also been done at the University of California, Davis, which appears to give 99% plus accuracy regarding dam and sire.

Female fertility

Females are normally bred for the first time between fifteen and twenty-four months of age. Dr. Walter Bravo, a Peruvian expert on llamas and alpacas, said that it's common to breed at one year or sixty percent of expected weight in South America. At one llama conference, he asked why North American breeders are waiting so long.

When we acquired our first llamas, the general attitude was that fertility problems were few and far between, not really anything to be too concerned about. They were estimated to be about two percent of the female llama population. Since then, people have realized that they occur with noticeably greater frequency than that.

One breeder estimated that about eighty percent of the females get pregnant easily and within a few weeks. Another recommended, ``If you have a herd of ten adult, producing females, think of eight babies a year.'' This percentage would take into account birthing problems as well as fertility problems. Other findings differ somewhat from these. We are still in the early stages of research.

According to one study of Peruvian llama herders, female llamas there tend to average around one offspring every other year. The herders did not expect any of them to give birth two years in a row. So even a good female might have no more than four to six offspring during her lifetime. Our situation here is very much more

It took many breedings to get Lil Bit pregnant.

prolific than that, as many females here have one baby a year, like clockwork, with no problems at all. The low South American fecundity is probably due in part to nutrition and to untreated uterine infections.

We had our problems with Lil Bit, but after several years of trying various things, she did eventually have a fine daughter. She has not gotten pregnant every year, but she has now had several babies.

Remember that the llama industry is really in its infancy in this country. The massive amounts of research done on other livestock just aren't matched. Several veterinary departments of state universities have research underway; probably the best-known are the University of California at Davis, Colorado State University, and Oregon State University. There is South American research as well, much of it on the alpaca.

If you find yourself with a female who isn't getting pregnant, talk it over thoroughly with your veterinarian, and find out what he or she suggests. In many cases, persistence and skill have paid off. Your vet may also know if there are any veterinary research centers where you could take your llama for further tests.

Don't give up hope. I heard about a supposedly infertile female who was purchased for very little and added to a pack string. The next year there was a baby. I can't help but wonder what kind of pandemonium she caused among the males while hiking. Bobra Goldsmith tells of a spayed female whom she trained to pack: "Although the veterinarians told me that she would not be attractive to males, when I took her on a training trip with two young males, they certainly knew she was a female llama. I had to keep her at the back of the line because they were orgling at her and would have jumped her." (Orgling is a particular sound made by male llamas when they are breeding.) Bobra knew of an infertile female who had packed very happily with a gelding. She added that another good use for an infertile female would be as a companion for a young female who might otherwise have to live alone.

You can avoid some fertility problems by only purchasing female llamas after they have undergone a thorough examination by a veterinarian. Many purchasers haven't done this, but it makes a lot of sense.

Jack and Dee Meyer have kept young females until they've had one daughter, then gotten them bred again and sold them at that point.

A bred female with one baby already born is worth more than a weanling. This approach also gave the Meyers a chance to fully evaluate each female's reproductive capacity and mothering abilities, plus they always had the option of keeping her line in their herd through that first daughter. The buyer gets a female with a proven track record. I like this approach.

Choosing a stud

When we bought our first llamas, the common practice was to buy a male and a female, not closely related to each other, and to breed them. Since the early 1980s, there has been a greater appreciation of the role of the male. Genetically, the male is more important than any one female, since you can have so many more offspring from him than from a female. Some studs are described as prepotent, that is, they throw their characteristics quite strongly.

When llama breeder Linda Rodgers visited many ranches in putting together her small herd, she was struck by how often a female who was ordinary in appearance produced beautiful babies if bred to a good stud whose qualities were complementary to hers. For that reason, and being on a small budget, Linda's strategy was to select sound but not spectacular females, and then breed to outstanding studs owned by other people. "Now, it's much easier," she told me. "For a few thousand dollars you can buy a nice male that might have gone for twenty thousand a few years ago. That saves you the risks and time of travelling. People may want to buy bred females at first, and take their time choosing studs. Tastes do change. You can often get free breedings included in the price of a female, too."

If you want to avail yourself of other people's studs, be sure to select one registered with the ILR. The arrangements vary. Typically, the female is transported to the ranch where the male is. Females are often re-bred about two weeks after giving birth, so she may have her baby with her. Some breeders will trade back and forth with each other's studs.

Be sure to find out what the fee includes. Does it cover as many breedings as necessary to get the female pregnant no matter what, or only routine breeding, excluding fertility problems with your female? Does it include the right to bring a different female if your first one turns out to be infertile? What kind of pregnancy testing will be done, and who will pay for it? Live birth guarantees are becoming more customary. Does the fee include boarding costs of your llama while it is at someone else's farm? If there happen to be veterinary costs, these are more commonly paid by the llama's owner. Incidentally, many breeders insure female llamas when they are taking them away from home.

Dan and Marilyn Milton of Highland Llamas are well-known, especially in the western United States, for their travelling stud service. They travelled thousands of miles with their Chilean import, Bogart, and his sons. Some other owners of studs are doing this too. As a small breeder emotionally attached to my ladies, I've never been very enthusiastic about taking them someplace else for breeding, at the most exciting time of year, right when their babies are so much fun to watch! Not to mention that going on the road and to another ranch carries some risk. For these reasons, we used Bogart very happily once when we had two open females, each with a baby by her side, whom we wanted to breed to somebody new.

If the breeders you are planning to use have a breeding contract, study it. It will most likely name the animals, specify that you have a recent veterinary certificate of health for your female as well as proof of registration with the International Lama Registry. It should state the fee, whether any part of it is nonrefundable, and when it is due. It should specify a boarding fee, if there is one, and who will pay any veterinary bills that arise. It should state the guarantee, if there is one; if it guarantees, for example, a live birth, it should also indicate what the choices are if the baby is aborted or stillborn. If there isn't a contract, it would be a good idea to write something up, since there are so many things that could be interpreted differently.

In choosing a stud for breeding, ask to see his babies. Find out if there are any known genetic defects in his parentage and in his offspring. Also, it might not occur to you to ask if he has had knee surgery! Since crooked legs can be corrected by surgery, this is sometimes done. If the breeder says yes, I wouldn't breed to that stud, because crooked knees is a trait that can be inherited.

"We used outside breedings exclusively in our first four years. With a dozen outside breedings behind us, I still have mixed feelings about doing it," Carroll Albert told me. "There are some real advantages. You are using a stud who has successfully demonstrated his ability to produce desirable traits on a number of females, you get in on the coattails of a highly promoted stud, and you can expand the genetic diversity of your herd. We found that a considerable side benefit was the depth of knowledge that the more experienced llama breeders shared generously with us.

"But we're also aware of the inherent risks, to mother and baby, of travel, new physical environment, new herd social structure, potential exposure to infection, and stress. All contribute to health concerns. We're relieved that we are now in a position to use our own studs on our farm for the bulk of our breedings."

In recent years, a tremendous number of good quality males have become available, so even little ranches can have multiple studs. Say that in your first year, your stud breeds to your females, and those babies are born in the second year. When any of them are ready to breed in another year and a half or so, you will need access to another stud, as you wouldn't breed them to their father.

On the other hand, it's quite common for breeders who live near each other to trade studs, and that can save on any possible management problems from having males that can't get along, as well as on expenses.

If you breed with your own stud, be sure he's old enough. Although a young male may begin trying to mount females in his early weeks of life, his penis adheres to the prepuce, the fold of skin which covers it. This prevents him from fully extending the penis. The age at which a male is sexually mature ranges from sixteen months (and sometimes even younger) to three years.

Inexperienced males can slow up your breeding program. We bought an adult male who, the owner believed, had impregnated some females, though he had no babies on the ground yet and they hadn't done pregnancy testing. We weren't able to get this male to put his penis into the right place on the females; he was consistently riding too high, and he was less tolerant of our attempts to help than our other males were. Where Levi would be blissfully unaware of anything but breeding, Thundercloud was alert to every distraction. A man who was helping us jokingly imitated the orgling sound that male llamas make while they are breeding, and our stud turned his head around and spat on him.

We called the previous owners to see if they remembered the llama riding high; they said they did, and also that their females had turned out not to be pregnant. Finally, Linda Rodgers got Thundercloud to find the right place, partly by the use of a steep hillside. Once the llama discovered what he was supposed to do, he succeeded in impregnation, and has bred quite skillfully at every opportunity ever since.

Some studs seem to be more apt to throw male or female offspring. "We have had seventeen males born in a row," Cutler Umbach told me. "The odds against seventeen males in a row, assuming that you have a fifty-fifty chance just like flipping a coin and getting heads seventeen times in a row, are over four thousand to one. We took the male-producing stud out of service. I guess I buy into the model that it's the male that determines the gender of the offspring."

Male llamas who are used for breeding can also be used for packing, driving, showing, taking in parades, and so forth. There is not an enormous difference between an intact male and a gelding in either personality or performance. Llamas are quite different from horses in this respect. Lynn Hyder, whose herd sire Apple Jack has won many performance competitions, is a strong advocate of doing things with your studs. It's great public relations, and you get to know the animal much better. Bobra Goldsmith uses Jester, one of her main studs, for driving to cart. She has taken him to many parts of the country.

We noticed that around the time we were using our males for breeding, if we took them walking on our ranch or nearby for an hour or two, they would want to go back—showing this by humming or by trying to turn back. Sometimes they were quite insistent, and not fun to hike with. But if you take your animal away from home, usually the new environment interests him, and he puts aside thoughts of his ladies for a while. Carroll Albert takes her males on longer pack trips. She commented, "We learned to resign ourselves to an earful of humming the entire first day. After that, they settle into enjoying the trip!"

If you buy male llamas who turn out not to be good candidates for breeding, it's a good idea to have them gelded. This does make some difference in territoriality and inclination to fight. Gelding used to commonly be done at weaning. We now know that skeletal development is affected by gelding before two or three years of age, so waiting is advised.

Hereditary defects and inbreeding in llamas

The rate of birth defects in North American llamas concerns many people. Dr. LaRue W. Johnson, a llama researcher at Colorado State University, says, "I think breeders should make a serious effort to educate themselves about genetics...We have a small genetic pool here and a fair number of genetic defects." Dr. Murray E. Fowler of the University of California at Davis states, "Over eighty congenital/-hereditary defects are known in llamas and alpacas." (A congenital characteristic is one that an animal is born with.)

When recessive genes for defects are present in a population, inbreeding—breeding closely related animals, such as brother to sister or parent to offspring—makes it far more likely that an animal will inherit the recessive genes from both parents and thus be more likely to display the defect.

It is a common practice in animal breeding to breed distantly related animals to each other. If there are excellent characteristics in the animals, the hope is that the genes for them will be inherited. Linebreeding is the term for this practice. The question is, what is linebreeding and what is inbreeding?

Breeding two llamas who share one grandparent in common is probably the most widely used form of linebreeding. Some breeders advocate and practice linebreeding, but many consider linebreeding to be avoided in North American llamas, because of the already small gene pool.

The llamas that were imported from South America have made it easier for breeders to outcross, or breed animals from lines that have been geographically distinct in the recent past. As nothing much is known about the ancestry of the imported animals, there's a gamble there too. Now that many imported llamas have been here for some time, you can find out what they have produced.

Whatever form of breeding is used, there are inevitably some defective animals born. As the late Ben Huff pointed out at one of the International Llama Association conferences, with sheep or cattle, it's normal for the mistakes to be butchered and eaten. With llamas, what happens to the animals born genetically flawed as a result of inbreeding? In some of the animals, the flaws won't show, and they will be used for breeding stock; their offspring may or may not be flawed. But other animals will show their flaws. Some may need to be euthanized, while some can live as pets, depending on the seriousness of the condition. Of course, many inbred animals are not flawed.

Breeding for what?

Many breeders are utterly fascinated with the process of breeding for
an animal they envision. It's a long-term activity. As breeder Lynn
Hyder puts it, "Well, we come from the farm. You plant seeds in the
ground and you have to have patience that they're going to come up,
and you're going to take care of them, and maybe that fall you can
harvest a crop from them. And if you've got a breeding program
going, you're talking about years now. It took me seven years to see
the llama I was looking for."

Carroll Albert told me, "As a biologist, one of the greatest
thrills I get from llama breeding is in watching the interplay of genes
on the phenotype, or physical appearance, of the offspring. Certain
characteristics, like frame size, conformation, and wool length, are
traits which usually seem to manifest in the offspring somewhere
between the sire's phenotype and the dam's. Others like body color are
more difficult to predict, as are certain color markings that are
particularly appealing to us, like a white bib or a tuxedo and white
socks."

In selecting breeding stock and developing a breeding
program, what do you look for? There are considerations of both
temperament and conformation.

Temperament is very important. "You want a llama that retains
its llama aloofness and yet isn't flighty or uncomfortable with itself,"
Linda Rodgers commented. "People who are really into breeding are
very aware of temperament. New people often don't understand how
inherited temperament is. They don't realize how many extra hours of
labor difficult llamas can require—and it's easier on your body if a
llama is not a giant buckaroo!" I thought ruefully of a couple of the
first llamas we bought.

Conformation, or the build of an animal, is a major factor to
consider in a breeding program. First, the animals must be sound, that
is, free of defects. If you have experience at evaluating the
conformation of other animals, learning to apply it to llamas will be
easier than if you are starting from scratch. It's essential to learn. Visit
as many breeders as you can, and ask them to explain their ideas of
conformation.

Does the animal have a straight back and straight front legs?
Looking at an animal from the side, observe the angle of the back
legs, how much they curve back underneath the body. An animal with

too much curvature here is described as *sickle-hocked*, and is undesirable.

The reason straight front legs are important is that most of the weight of the llama rests on these legs. Animals with faults here may not be able to walk as well. They may not develop problems until later life, or never, but some of them will. While knock knees are often passed on genetically, they also can be the result of nutritional imbalance. During its first days of life, the legs of a baby llama may appear quite crooked. As it matures, at times its legs may look terrible and at other times they may appear quite straight. Eventually, the appearance becomes more consistent.

The llama industry does not have written, widely accepted standards, and many breeders don't want them, arguing that the standards would favor certain types of llamas over others. Llamas come in wonderfully diverse shapes and sizes, and there seem to be as many tastes among breeders as there are looks in llamas.

The Alpaca and Llama Show Association has developed a list of traits, both positive and negative, that are used in judging. The positive ones are worded rather generally, calling, for example for the llama to be "well proportioned, balanced, and symmetrical." The negative ones include leg deformations, jaw problems, external genital abnormalities, and so on. (A summary of this list is in Chapter Six.)

One llama owner who believes we need standards as a safeguard is Tom Stammer, who has judged sheep, cattle, hogs, and horses. He comments, "In other livestock industries, like at the California State Ram Sale, there's a sifting committee, made up of maybe three judges, sifting rams out if they have a bad leg and will not lead a productive life. Or if they have one testicle, or overshot or undershot teeth.

"The industry wants that sifting. When you buy a purebred ram, you want a ram that's going to give your herd many years of service. But at these llama auctions, a lot of duds are being sold. For example, it's not a minor condition for a llama to have such extremely crooked legs that she's not going to last. Each time a female is carrying a cria, she gets heavier, and her legs can start breaking down. There are all these safeguards in other livestock industries that aren't happening in llamas. I think we should get some of those standards—of soundness, not taste."

There are other considerations in breeding. There are lots of different shapes of ears. You may hear breeders speak of *banana ears*, which are ones with a graceful banana-like curve. Some ears are tipped, where the very top of the ear hangs down a little. Other people don't object to that. Famous or desirable bloodlines are also a factor in selecting llamas to breed.

Color of wool is another choice. White is very common, and handspinners like it. A true gray is quite rare, and thus desirable. Llamas come in various markings: paint, appaloosa, bay.

Breeders differ in the build they like. Some breeders like rather wide animals, and thick leg bone has some popularity. Breeder Bobra Goldsmith commented, "I'm much more concerned about defective legs than I am whether the bone is thin or thick. Arabian horses have fairly fine bones, and they are known for endurance. With llamas, it is possible that fine or average bone is denser than thick bone.

"I think that some of the conformation characteristics that people admire in llamas are appropriate more to other animals," she continued. "One aspect of llama conformation which tends to come from cattle breeders, and maybe even horse breeders, is the square blocked animal, with a wide chest.

"Llamas tend to be pacers, and as pacers if their body is narrow, the displacement of their weight from one side to the other is minimized. If you breed a very wide animal, he's going to be waddling because he has to transfer his weight from side to side. I am afraid we are breeding a new kind of llama whose build is not as functional for him as it would have been."

A small number of llamas have blue eyes. It's a trait that many breeders are careful to avoid, because in some other species, light blue eyes are associated with some undesirable conditions. This is true of horses, and llama breeders with a horse background are the ones most likely to avoid blue eyes. But both Dr. Julio Sumar of Peru and Dr. Julie Koenig of this country, well-known llama researchers, have stated publicly that there is no evidence of unsoundness in blue-eyed llamas. Dr. Sumar did say that in Peru they avoid breeding llamas with pink skin around the eyes and mouth, as those animals seemed more disposed to skin diseases. He added that there is some correlation between blue eyes and pink skin.

It seems that breeding a blue-eyed female to a male with dark eyes would make it unlikely that the offspring would be blue-eyed. The trait seems to be more accepted in alpacas, where white wool is desirable. The genetics are not yet fully known, but there does seem to be a correlation between light blue eyes and white wool.

A highly desirable quality in a llama for breeding is an indefinable presence: this is partly a matter of how all the llama's parts are put together, and partly a matter of its personality.

On any given point, tastes vary. What kind of ears do you like? How much wool on the head? When is a llama knock-kneed? One person's charming petite woolly llama is another person's hedgehog on toothpicks. I've heard more than one discussion get very heated; these matters bear on how easily you can sell your llamas and for what prices.

As you visit farms, develop your own breeding plan: it may change, but think about it before you select your first animals. Begin with breeding for sound conformation, good disposition, and good health (no genetic defects or fertility problems known in the animal or in its ancestors, so far as you can determine). Then think of other factors. What do you care about?

Breeding for long or short wool

Since the mid-1980s, llamas with long wool have become popular. They have been extensively promoted; most of the full-color ads in llama publications show this type of animal. This popularity has greatly influenced the breeding of llamas in this country. For many people, wool became the overwhelmingly important standard. Fortunately, some people have always also been concerned with soundness.

The graceful, flowing wool can be very lovely. Some llama breeders came to llamas with a background in spinning, raising other fiber animals, or fiber arts. Some of these people are quite active in using llama wool, breeding for the kind of woolly llamas they desire, and educating others to look at the fibers in terms of fineness, luster, and crimp. As the llama wool industry matures, more breeders will pay attention to the utility of the wool as well as how it looks on the animal. The fashion for woolly heads, ears, and back legs has nothing to do with spinning, as wool from those parts of the body is not normally spun.

I initially had trouble understanding the popularity of the woollier llamas, as I didn't find them more beautiful than the elegant lines of classical llamas. But then I heard something at an

Many breeders love long, graceful wool.

Some woolly llamas have cascading leg wool.

International Llama Association conference: Leo K. Bustad of the Delta Society, an organization interested in the human-animal bond, explained the concept of neoteny. "Konrad Lorenz proposed that a high and bulging forehead, a large brain case compared to the face, along with large eyes and rounded cheeks and small size with stubby limbs aroused the nurturing response and elicited tender feelings for such attractive objects." Many breeds of dogs have been neotenized. Bustad suggests that llamas also fit parts of this description. So this human tendency to neotenize may account for some of the popularity of llamas and especially of many "super-woollies," who are often cuter—thus evoking more of a nurturing instinct in us—than the less woolly ones.

Tom Stammer travels extensively in South America for his business, and he is troubled by the changing North American look. "When I go to Peru, I look at what llamas really look like. They're meant for packing. They're tall, and there's just not wool coming out all over them. I looked at a recent *Llamas* and one from the mid-1980s, and you could already see the difference in the advertising pictures, of what we're breeding for."

One major breeder who is also a commercial packer, Steve

Rolfing, told me, "I am breeding for four hundred pound, narrow-chested, long-legged pack llamas, with a long fine coat of wool. I believe we can breed a quality of wool equal to the alpacas. If you don't want to pack with it, just cut it off."

He continued, "I don't see the need to have two different breeds of llamas, the small wool-producers and the non-woolly packers. To me the most beautiful animal has the characteristics of both types. It's the hardest to produce—it may take us twenty years—but it's a lofty goal."

Personally, I stand with the fans of the classic llama. While I wish Steve Rolfing and others with that goal well, I would very much hate to see the classic llamas die out because of the rampant popularity of wool. In the past, many breeders felt that they had to breed for wool to make the kind of money they wanted. Now that the llama market is becoming more diverse, maybe it will be easier for people who like the classic llamas to breed them.

CHAPTER FOUR:

Birthing

WHENEVER THE TIME for delivery drew near, we watched our ladies closely. Their field came right up to the house, next to my study, so I could be working inside and observing their activities. Posey liked to sit just under my study window.

Finally, something would be a little different. Posey would be up and down, up and down, for a couple of hours. Juliet might hum, in a grumbling kind of way. My concentration on anything else would dwindle. I'd trim my fingernails, double-check the contents of our birthing bag, postpone trips to town. Juliet, our second female and one who had already had several babies when we got her, fooled me a couple of times. Her muscles weren't as tight as Posey's. I'd see flashes of hot pink from the inner tissues of her vulva when she lay down. I'd decide the birth was about to happen, and once again postpone the trip to town. It could go on like this for days.

Our first birth was perfect. The baby was born quickly, stood up immediately, and was soon nursing. It was Posey's first baby, and she handled it as if she had been doing it all her life. We were thrilled, all the more so as it was just in time for description and photos to go into my first book, *Living with Llamas*, about to go to press.

A few months later, I found Juliet with a baby half out of her. It wasn't moving, and the moment I saw its eyes I knew something was wrong. The vet thought the little one had been dead for about a day. The next day, three thousand copies of *Living with Llamas* were delivered. I was very excited about the book, but I couldn't stop thinking about how thin the veil is between life and death, and not just for baby llamas. Juliet looked for her baby for days, sniffing my sheepskin boots with great interest until I stopped wearing them into the barn.

Posey's next baby was out in a flash, but didn't start nursing. After some hours, we had to milk out Posey, who screamed her protests. We didn't know how to tube-feed the little guy, so we bottle-fed him for three days. Kelly later called those days the three hardest days of our long marriage. We couldn't agree on timing or strategy. It didn't help that a heat wave was going on, the barn was full of flies, and there was dry thunder and lightning every evening in the mountains all around us.

On the fourth morning, I lifted my head from the pillow, looked out the window into the pasture, and saw the baby nursing. It was a glorious sight. He and Posey had been drifting apart

Lil Bit finally had a daughter.

emotionally, but as soon as nursing began, their bonding resumed. Later, we gelded him just in case he had bonded too much with us. We doubted that he had, but knew of another little fellow who had bonded in two days of bottle-feeding and later did develop some behavior problems. Posey's baby turned out fine.

It was almost a year later that Juliet was due again. She was up and down interminably, groaning a lot, on one of those nasty spring days when the ground is thoroughly muddy and the rain changes to snow and back again several times an hour.

A foot appeared. The other foot didn't. We had moved Juliet into the barn. Kelly pointed out that I had smaller hands than he. My clipped fingernails came in handy, as—my heart racing—I washed up, put on surgical gloves, and reached into Juliet. Mercifully, the other foot was right there, just twisted back a little. It was easy to manoeuver. I was glad to have the experience, and so relieved that I didn't even care when it was another boy and we hadn't had any girls yet in three years of births.

A few minutes later, Kelly took another look and discovered that what I'd thought was the penis was just a marking. We looked under the tail. There was a long vertical tab. We had our first female! I felt like an idiot, but a happy one. I knew I wasn't the first llama owner to make a mistake about a baby's sex.

Late that afternoon, we brought mother and baby from the soggy barn to the rock-floored part of our living room for a while, so they could dry out, but also just for pure pleasure. Juliet watched and we watched as young Blossom skittered around the uneven floor. We were all content.

Starting with that baby, we had girl after girl, each one healthy, adorable, and easily born. Our fields were full of baby girls running at sunset. Even Lil Bit, who hadn't gotten pregnant in several years of trying, got pregnant and stayed pregnant.

There was Pocahontas, Posey's first daughter, who was up and nursing right away. The next year, we had three babies due. First came Lally, daughter of Lil. Three weeks later, Posey produced a beautiful little girl, Renaissance. We had tickets to go hear the Paul Winter Consort that evening, and little Renny popped out in the late afternoon. She nursed, the placenta was passed, and we got to the concert just in time, our hearts full as the lovely music swirled around us. Soon Juliet gave birth to Harmony, Blossom's full sister. What treasures in our pastures! We spent a lot of time watching the little girls play.

By the next year, we had sold Juliet and Lil wasn't pregnant. Blossom had a stillbirth. It was sad, but we were learning a deeper acceptance of the ways of nature. Just as we were deciding to move to town, Posey gave birth to another daughter, whom we named Perestroika. She was the fifth female our stud Levi had sired, and he had no sons. To think that we had almost gelded him once!

Like many llama owners, we had never before bred any animals. We weren't prepared for the emotional intensity of birthing. But as time went on, we did gain some equanimity. When Lally didn't nurse at first, we felt much less stress than we had the first time that had occurred. We bottle-fed her a little, and soon she found her mother. I attended at Harmony's birth when Kelly was out of town; the vet did later tease me about how many phone calls I'd made to him.

I have heard estimates that about ten percent of all births might have one problem or another, minor or large. Our rate was higher than that. I know, from talking to other breeders, that we had more problems than the average. I know a couple who have had over twenty births, with only a few, extremely minor problems. Another breeder has had over thirty-five births without stillbirths or premature babies; only once was a female slow to get pregnant.

In creating the spreadsheets in Chapter Ten, I devised a figure called the *thriving baby rate*. It subtracts from 100% the percentage of times a female doesn't get pregnant and the percentage of stillbirths and babies who die. Primarily due to Lil's not getting pregnant at first, our thriving baby rate was very low: Of the seventeen possible babies that could have been born and thrived in our herd in the first eight years, only nine—which is 53%—did. This is a good example of how the success of very small herds is more vulnerable to the toss of the dice than is the success of a larger herd, where things tend to average out. But our misfortune during that time was greatly mitigated by having far more thriving females than males.

What is a normal thriving baby rate? We need more statistics to know, but several experienced breeders have suggested doing your planning based on around eighty percent.

Some of our mishaps were due to our inexperience and to the newness of the llama industry in North America. The baby that Juliet lost may have been because she was considerably overweight. She was overweight when we bought her—which I hadn't fully realized—and we hadn't taken the measures needed to get her weight down.

The bottle feeding might have been avoided if we, and the people we consulted, had known things that are known now—especially that shoving a baby under the dam often doesn't work! The baby tends to resist, rather than to notice the teats you're trying to introduce. During the 1980s, many breeders were separating the mothers from the rest of the herd before the birth, but now some are letting the mothers stay with the herd. They feel that this creates a situation less stressful for the animals and less conducive to the babies trying to nurse from the walls of the barn.

If you decide to breed llamas, there is a lot you can do to prepare yourself. In selecting females to purchase, ask about their mothers' birthing histories. You can inform yourself about birthing by attending conferences, reading, and watching videotapes. Well-known llama veterinarian Dr. LaRue Johnson does an excellent clinic on birthing, which he often presents in conjunction with llama conferences. We made a video of his clinic, with some video of births inserted; see the order form at the end of the book. Other people often provide birthing information at conferences. A book I've already recommended, *Caring for Llamas: A Health and Management Guide*, has a chapter on newborn llamas.

You may be able to find llama breeders in your area who will act as your mentor at first, available to answer your questions and maybe give you a hand. Perhaps they can call you when they think a birth is about to happen at their place. Breeder Linda Rodgers comments, "There's no substitute for actually seeing a birth!"

You can carefully select your veterinarian. How accessible, how informed about llamas, and how quick to act in a potential emergency, he or she is can make a difference. You should also select one or more back-up veterinarians, in case yours is on vacation or is out for the day on a ranch many miles away.

Many people who own a few female llamas also have full-time jobs. If you can't be home, perhaps a neighbor can keep an eye out, or someone can drop by now and then.

I don't recommend entering into breeding glibly. It's not for everybody. I'm very glad for the births we had. I learned a lot about llamas, about myself, and about life—especially from the hard times.

Juliet is just about to give birth.

About an hour later.

And there are few things that have delighted my heart more than a new little llama running around the pasture, in its first hours out here in the air with the rest of us.

Basics of birthing

Female llamas carry their young for an average gestation time of eleven and a half months, but there is quite a lot of variation. Eleven months is common, and some llamas have gone more than a year. First-time mothers often go longer than others.

Some females never look very pregnant, and then suddenly there's a baby. Others look like you could land an airplane on their backs, to use Bobra Goldsmith's phrase, for the last few weeks. If you've owned a female for several years and have a record of exact breeding dates so that you know how long she has carried previous babies, you may have a pretty close idea of when the birth is due. Even then, the baby can surprise you. There's also a great variation in when the dam's teats begin to enlarge. It may be a month before birth, or it could even be just after the birth.

There are almost never twins, once in several thousand births. A llama baby is usually just called a baby, though often people use the word 'cria,' Spanish for any baby animal.

Llamas typically give birth in the daylight hours, which certainly is nice for the humans involved. There's an interesting evolutionary reason. In the high Andes of South America, as in any high mountains, the daytime temperatures are much warmer than the nighttime ones. Furthermore, during the time of year that most llama babies are born, there are often thunderstorms in the afternoon. So the babies born in the mornings had warmer temperatures to dry out and start nursing in, and thus a better chance of surviving.

Births do occur at night, now and then. Llama owners who thought it was a sure thing that it would be in the daytime have sometimes been surprised to find newborns from the night. Lately, several breeders have observed that more births seem to be happening at night.

"We had one that I found in the middle of the night," Bill Barnett told me. "It was a first time mother, and my wife Gail had been watching her. I'd been gone. The llama had been breaking off from the herd for a few days, but not that much. She'd mix back with the herd again. Gail watched her every hour or two. The last time she checked her was around 9:30 at night, and the mother seemed normal and was just lying with the rest of the animals. When I came home around one in the morning, I had a premonition. I knew she was close, and I went out there. That baby was just lying there like a dummy. He'd been born for at least an hour, and the mother was lying about ten feet away, exhausted. She must have had a difficult labor. I would have lost that baby if I hadn't gone out."

The birth itself usually goes rather quickly, though you may not think so at the time. Often the female is standing; sometimes she lies down. She doesn't usually need assistance from you, but many people like to be present, to assist if necessary. Some breeders prefer to leave the llama alone, and watch from a distance with binoculars. Typically the nose and feet come out first. Once the front legs are out a bit, some breeders may pull gently downward on them, only in rhythm with the contractions, just to make it a little easier for the mother. Sometimes it helps to rotate the shoulders. It's often helpful to milk out the mother's teats, to be sure she has milk. There can be a waxy plug on her nipples, and if it's removed it's that much easier for the baby. Also, the smell of milk on the teats will attract the baby toward them. During labor, you can reach under the mother, and she may scarcely notice. I've been impressed with how little our females are bothered by our messing around with them while they're giving birth, even those who normally dislike being handled.

In a normal birth, the baby starts breathing right away. We clear away any bits of the amniotic sac that might be near the baby's nostrils and mouth.

It's important to dip the end of the baby's umbilical cord in 7% iodine as soon as possible, to protect against infection. Never pour iodine into the cord, as it could go up into the body and do great harm. (It's a good idea to double-check the umbilical cord about an hour later, to make sure it isn't bleeding.) Some breeders give injections at this time. If it's cold, you may want to dry the baby off a bit, with towels or a hair dryer on a low setting. The mother llamas do not have an instinct to lick their babies.

So the newborn is flopping around on the ground, covered with pieces of the sac it comes in, not yet fluffily cute. Its mother may be sniffing it. If you haven't separated the mother, every llama in the field is gathered around, trying to sniff the baby. They're all excited. You are trying to douse the navel with iodine while getting a good look at the baby's belly. Do you have a male or a female? The two sexes are born in roughly equal quantities.

Some of our babies have been scrambling to get up immediately; others have been more relaxed about it. And these first actions have often seemed characteristic of the personalities that we came to know later. All our full-term babies have been on their feet within a few minutes to maybe half an hour.

Soon their wobbly walking turns to wobbly running, and then they are prancing around like they'd been doing it forever! They only run into the fence once or twice before they learn to avoid it. I feel awe at how much these little newborns know. When Lally was born, some friends living on our ranch had a human baby the same week. It was striking to see the two infants together.

Llama babies are usually successfully nursing within a few hours. Every breeder is relieved when a baby starts nursing, as it's extremely important for the little one's immunity to disease that it receive the colostrum, or first milk, from the mother. You may want to have a back-up plan with your veterinarian or another local llama owner if there should be a problem. And if you ever have a stillbirth, do milk out the mother's colostrum and put it in the freezer for possible future use. It's a good idea to keep 30 to 40 ounces of backup colostrum—either goat or cow—in your freezer. It should be from a first milking, and it will keep about a year.

Within a few hours of birth, the mother passes the placenta. Stretch it out on the ground someplace, to make sure that it's all there. When Juliet had a stillbirth, part of the placenta remained in her. That called for the veterinarian to remove it and administer antibiotics. We bury the placentas, fairly deeply and in a place where they wouldn't attract dogs.

Normal birth weights range from about twenty-two to thirty-five pounds. Babies weighing less may be premature, and should be monitored carefully. We weigh the baby by holding it in our arms and weighing human plus llama on a level bathroom scale. Many llama owners use special scales. We prefer to weigh the babies right away, because after even half an hour, we've found some of the mothers to be much less appreciative of our presence. Posey, never slow to spit, has really blasted us a couple of times when we approached her baby an hour or so after birth.

Newborns call for some care in the early days of their life.

Many breeders weigh the babies daily for a week or two, to verify continued weight gain; Linda Rodgers comments, "It's the only way you know whether the mother has enough milk or not." They may check to be sure the mother is producing milk on all four teats, and the baby is actually getting it. They may watch to be sure the baby urinates and defecates normally; and they watch to be sure the baby's behavior indicates it's thriving: it's active, bright-eyed, and nursing. They provide special shelter in hot or cold weather. Generally, people try to schedule births for the nicest weather, but this isn't always possible.

Thinking about birthing evokes a kaleidoscope of images and feelings in me. As the baby emerges from the mother, it resembles bagpipes, with those long, long legs sticking every which way. The babies begin reaching up for the nipple, often curving their necks before they are standing. They use llama language gestures, such as putting their ears back, immediately. And I think of my deep sense of contentment in the days when there's a new baby to care for, giggle over, and cherish.

CHAPTER FIVE

Buying and Selling Llamas

THE LLAMAS OF NORTH AMERICA await you. Standing in their pastures or at auction, there are llamas for sale in every region: from farms and ranches, sometimes at cooperative sales, and at auctions. Read the llama periodicals for classified ads placed by llama owners as well as for announcements of auctions. Before you grab your checkbook and go, take some time to plan.

Buying llamas at ranches

What are you looking for in llamas? You might make a list of what you want. If you are buying an adult, consider its whole history. How good a mother is that bred female? Does that stud have babies on the ground, and what are they like?

How many llamas are you looking for at first? Many llama breeders advise starting with just two, and seeing how well you like them before going further. A solitary llama is likely to be unhappy.

Take plenty of time on conformation. Ken Safley gave me a tip on how to tell if an animal is knock-kneed: "Squat down behind the animal and look clear through to the front legs. You can tell whether it's knock-kneed or not, because the inside of the front legs normally doesn't have wool on it."

As well as all the specific details, there are intangibles. "When I look at llamas," Bill Barnett said, "I look at their presence, color of their wool, and the way they hold themselves. Then I start to go about analyzing the conformation and the physical health."

Bill and several others recommended taking a friend or a consultant with you when you are considering purchasing an animal.

Looking at lots of llamas will train your eye.

Susan Torrey, who has long enjoyed raising llamas and has acted as a consultant, commented, "I encourage people to look and look and look. Especially for newcomers, the more you look, the happier you're going to be with what you finally purchase, and the more you'll learn about llamas."

How are you going to find llamas for sale? Many llama associations offer free lists of breeders. It's worthwhile to join one or more of these groups, not least for the membership directory which lists all the members. This gives you access to everyone, not just the people who paid to be on the breeders' list. Close to half of all ILA members, for example, have five or fewer female llamas.

ILA, the largest organization, has numerous regional affiliates. An easy way to start making contacts in your area is to call the head of the regional group. I do recommend calling rather than writing, since it takes a lot of the other person's time to write you back, and people who love to be outdoors with their animals are not always the best at staying on top of paperwork!

If you just want to look at llamas and don't really know if you will be buying some, describe your situation to the breeder. Many farms do show their llamas to people who might buy someday. Some don't.

You may run into the 'barn-blind' seller, or seller who genuinely believes that the animal being offered is of better quality than it is. This is partly because of the newness of the llama industry and the large number of people who haven't owned livestock before.

It's easy to fall in love with the first llamas you see, but do look around some; inform yourself about current prices. Pay attention to the people as well as the animals. Jack Meyer advises, "I think llama breeding is probably one of the more ethical businesses. But like anything that involves substantial amounts of money, it does attract those who are not so ethically minded. People should be cautious when they are out looking. A face-to-face meeting is always the best way."

Carroll Albert comments, "I suppose the ethics of llama owners run the full spectrum, but at the overwhelming majority of ranches we've visited, people have been open, honest, and ready to share. One of the wonderful things about raising llamas is getting to know the marvelous people involved."

Visiting individual farms is time-consuming but very rewarding. You will learn a lot from talking to a variety of people and looking at a lot of different animals.

Also find out about cooperative and consignment sales in your area. These are becoming more common. In many regions, local breeders have created pamphlets with maps to the different locations and perhaps an updated list of animals for sale. Your local classified ad shopper or local newspaper may yield some ads as well.

Veterinary checks

If you get seriously interested in one or more llamas, it's time for a vet check. You can use the seller's veterinarian, or you may prefer to use another vet in the area, to avoid putting the seller's vet in any position of conflict of interest. This hasn't bothered me, either as a buyer or a seller. I figured that the veterinarian who handled the herd would know things that might not be picked up by another person.

Certainly when the animal is worth thousands of dollars, it just makes sense to pay a modest fee for a vet check. If you are purchasing full mortality insurance, you will need a vet check. But even when you are buying an inexpensive male or two, you are going to be putting such a large emotional investment into the animals that I highly recommend you go to the trouble of having a vet check. The seller can be the nicest, most honest person in the world and still not know something that a veterinarian's exam will reveal.

If you decide on an animal, you may want to put a deposit on it subject to a satisfactory veterinary exam within so many days. It's desirable to have a purchase agreement, listing the price, a description of the animal and its ILR registration number, as well as any agreements or understandings, such as that the weanling will be trained to accept the halter and load into a vehicle before the day it's sold. If you are buying an animal meant to be used for breeding, it should say whether breeding capacity is guaranteed or not. See the two-page sidebar for one example of a purchase agreement. It's included for your convenience, but as with any legal papers, it would be prudent to have your attorney help you create one that suits your situation. This form is derived from one written by Bob Mallicoat, llama breeder and attorney, and shared at an ILA conference. You are welcome to use or modify it. It isn't guaranteed to be perfect!

Even if you don't draw up and sign a written form, looking over the one in the book can bring to the surface things that you should talk about with the seller. Some sellers prefer to receive cashier's checks, especially if they don't already know you and you're spending a lot of money. Among people who know each other, personal checks are also used.

Any guarantees?

Traditionally, in most livestock situations, breeding capacity has not been guaranteed. But the situation in llamas is rather different. Many breeders do offer guarantees. Terry Price, who is an attorney as well as the editor of *Llama Life*, wrote an article in which he strongly advocated that people should guarantee their animals, on both legal and ethical grounds. He pointed out that this has been done in some auction situations, and he suggests that the llama associations could create codes of ethics that their members would have to follow. In the meantime, he suggests breeders can keep their females until they have had one baby and successfully nursed it; that would leave no doubt that the animal had breeding capability.

Dr. Ralph Uber, who breeds both llamas and alpacas, comments that he would replace an animal with one of equal value or return the buyers' money, if a weanling grew up to be infertile. He hasn't had to, though. "Unfortunately, the majority of sellers will not make that guarantee. They say when you buy the animal, it's yours when you take it out the gate. I really don't think that's entirely fair. There should be some kind of cushion for the buyer."

"We sell our animals with a reproductive guarantee, even the weanlings," Carroll Albert said. "We feel that the considerable benefits to ourselves as sellers outweigh the potential risk of having to refund a purchase price someday. For one thing, as buyers, we found ourselves returning again and again to the same ranches over the years, because of the deep sense of trust we have for the owners' integrity. They are assured of our repeat business, partly because we know they stand behind their animals. As sellers, we feel the risk is reduced by knowing the reproductive capacity of our animal's lines."

Fred Bauer considered two different situations. "When people buy from me, I want them to be satisfied with their purchase. If a pre-existing condition turns up later that causes lack of reproductive ability, then I'll replace the animal. For instance, every now and then you hear about a female that doesn't have all her parts. Well, if I were to sell one as a breeder for thousands of dollars, I'll make good on it if she turns out not to have all her parts. If, on the other hand, I sell a male as a stud and three years later they say, 'Well, he's sterile,' in

Date:_____

AGREEMENT FOR THE SALE/PURCHASE OF A LLAMA

I/we hereby sell, assign, and transfer to _____ (buyer) all right, title, and interest in and to that certain live male/female (strike one) llama named _____ (name)' International Lama Registry Registration No. _____ (number)' sired by _____ (sire's name and ILR number) and born of _____ (mother's name and ILR number) on _____ (date of birth)' for the sum of $_____ (price)' to be paid as follows:_____

_____.

The purpose of this sale is to provide:

_____ A breedable female with/without (strike one) warranty.

_____ A bred female with _____(date) as the approximate date of breeding.

_____ A breedable male with/without (strike one) warranty.

_____ A gelded male.

_____ A healthy weaned male/female (strike one) with/without (strike one) warranty as to ultimate breeding capacity.

_____ No warranty of any kind.

_____ A trained llama possessing the following abilities:

_____

_____

Buyer/seller (strike one) will provide Veterinarian's certificate of good health and sound condition based upon examination within _____ (number) days of date of sale. Any monies received by Seller from Buyer shall be refunded if the Veterinarian's report is unsatisfactory to Buyer.

The Seller will provide the Buyer with records of the llama's history.

For a llama sold with warranty as breedable: Buyer will promptly provide breeding opportunity, and will maintain accurate and complete records. In the event the subject llama fails to breed within _____ (number) months of the date of sale, and after appropriate veterinary examination and treatment if required, Buyer shall notify Seller and provide Seller with a complete copy of the llama's record. Buyer shall have the option to return the subject llama to Seller with a proper bill of sale within _____ (time period) at Buyer's expense and to receive from Seller a full refund of the price paid, or another llama acceptable to Buyer within _____ (number) months, chosen from those llamas Seller is willing to offer.

(Strike out any option that does not apply.)

For a llama sold with warranty as a bred female: If the subject llama is found not to be pregnant by recognized examination procedures, or if no/no live (strike one) offspring is born of the subject llama within the anticipated remaining gestation period plus 30 days, Buyer shall notify Seller and have the option of returning the llama, at Buyers expense, to Seller for rebreeding, or of having the Seller return the sum of $_____ (amount) stud fee. Should all efforts to breed the llama, including veterinary examination and treatment if required, prove unsuccessful after ____-(number) months from date of sale, upon return of the llama to Seller, Buyer shall be entitled to a full refund of the price paid or another mutually acceptable llama to be delivered within ____(number) months. If buyer and seller do not agree on another llama, the purchase price shall be refunded.

For all llamas: Any additional contingencies or conditions of this sale as agreed to by all parties are as follows: (If none, so state.)

In the event of a dispute which the Buyer and the Seller cannot resolve together, the laws of the State of _____-(name) shall be controlling, and the dispute shall be submitted to arbitration under the rules of the American Arbitration Association. An award may be entered in any court having competent jurisdiction, and the prevailing party shall be entitled to reasonable attorney's fees in addition to costs.

This agreement shall inure to the benefit of and be binding upon the parties hereto and their respective next-of-kin, legatees, personal representatives, executors, legal representatives, successors, and permitted assigns.

In witness whereof the parties hereto have executed this Agreement on the day and year first written above.

------------------------------   ------------------------------
Seller   Buyer

------------------------------   ------------------------------
Seller   Buyer

A sample purchase agreement.

that case, unless they can show me that it was pre-existing, I would probably not replace him simply because there are so many things that can happen in that three years to cause sterility, like a high fever."

I am pleased that more breeders are offering reproductive guarantees, but whether there is a guarantee or not seems to me to be a reasonable thing for the buyer and the seller to negotiate. There are circumstances in which people may be selling an animal because they need the money or need to get out of llamas entirely. Not everybody has the cash flow to permit them to let several thousand dollars sit in a savings account or other liquid investment until the youngster has grown up and gotten pregnant. If they had to offer the guarantee, in many cases they'd be wiser to just keep the llama until she was pregnant and then sell her. There are knowledgeable buyers who would be quite willing to take the risk, especially for a lower price on the animal.

Buying at auctions

Fred Hartman, who has been active in promoting exotic breeds of cattle for many years, began llama auctions. As the llama industry grew, several llama breeders have started putting on auctions as well. Some of these auctions have been extremely well done, and have become very popular gatherings for the llama community. They have also attracted new buyers. The Firecracker in Oregon and the Celebrity are the best known. A significant percentage of llamas are now sold via auctions.

We've only bid once at a llama auction. We had been talking about getting another stud, but we were in no hurry. At one auction, I noticed a llama who was my kind of animal. He had good bloodlines, and his wool was short enough for packing but longer than my other studs had. I liked his conformation. He was a little on the short side, but we've always liked small llamas.

Best of all, he had a special presence about him. He was quite calm despite numerous other male llamas in stalls around him. I felt intuitively that the animal might be right for us. I also felt that he might be a bargain here, where so many woollier studs were also for sale. And I love bargains, when they really are what I want. Kelly liked the llama too.

His owners were nearby, and kindly answered all our questions. They let us take him out for a long walk around the fairgrounds.

We had spotted him the day before the auction, so Kelly and I had time to sleep on it. We hadn't had a veterinarian's check, but we had looked him over as thoroughly as we could by ourselves, and he'd had a basic vet check to get his travel papers from out of state. The animal's breeding capacity was as yet unproven; he had no babies on the ground. We decided to spend up to a certain amount, knowing that it was a gamble. Could we get him for that? We'd just have to see.

The auction started. Our fellow's half-brother, winner of the show the day before and a much woollier llama, sold for forty thousand dollars. I gulped. Our agreed-upon limit was around a tenth of that.

The show winners sold, and the females, and finally they got down to the regular males. Pretty soon, out came the one we were going to bid on. I knew he wasn't really everyone's cup of tea. He wouldn't appeal to anyone breeding for long wool. Besides, the crowd had thinned out a lot.

There he was in the ring, and I was bidding. So were other people. Every now and then I nodded my head. It wasn't that easy to keep track of who had bid last. Did people ever bid up their own prices? I nodded again. I was suddenly very aware that the price at an auction is decided when the next-to-last person decides to drop out. I wasn't dropping out, at least not yet. "Sold," someone said. Thundercloud was ours, and for only fifteen hundred dollars. When we went back to the stall afterward, the sellers seemed rather glum. Evidently they too had thought he would sell for more.

We took him home and had a vet check before letting him near the rest of our herd. His health was fine.

This llama did turn out to have a problem that I've discussed in the chapter on breeding: he was positioning himself too high on the females when trying to breed. (Eventually he learned what to do.) His owners didn't know of this problem at the time; they gave us all the information they had themselves.

I think that the late placement in the auction worked in our favor. Some months before that, Chuck Forest had told me how his wife Joanne and a friend had purchased one of their studs at an auction. "They showed him to some other people there, who couldn't believe they'd gotten him for twenty-one hundred dollars. Well, he was placed at the very end of the auction. Everybody had left and they were watching. They had done their research." I hadn't forgotten that story.

"I like auctions," Averill Abbott told me. "I have been dissatisfied with a price I've gotten, but I had the choice. And if you buy an animal at an auction, you've got to be prepared to get somebody's junk. You need to know what you're looking for, or what to ask. You need to know what you're doing."

As for getting somebody else's junk, Dr. LaRue Johnson told in *Llama Life* of seeing an infertile female bought at auction. He had seen her three times, each time with a different owner. "Each time I have had to tell the new owner that this female was a hopeless fertility case. Some people won't or can't afford to cut their losses. Instead they send defective animals back to an auction!"

A while back, a friend and I were flipping through an auction catalog. My friend stopped to read closely the text advertising a particular llama. I looked at it too. "See those parents?" my friend asked. "They are brother and sister. I know the farm. The male jumped the fence. I remember when it happened, and the dates are right."

Taking part in an auction can be confusing. You need to be able to assess animals rapidly; if you have visited some ranches before you go to an auction, you will be in a better position to evaluate the animals. Things happen quickly: it can be hard to understand the auctioneer through the sound system, you may lose track of the bidding. It's helpful to have an experienced friend or acquaintance advising you at first.

Auctions are a significant part of the way llamas are bought and sold. For all buyers, there is some element of risk, lessened when they know the seller's integrity and when they know something about assessing llamas.

But auctions are a realm where llama owners are putting a lot of creativity and hard work; the risks to buyer, seller, and llama may be lessened in the future. Llama auctions seem to be evolving to a higher form of exchange. For example, sellers may offer reproductive guarantees, and buyers are becoming more knowledgeable.

What do llamas cost?

At this writing, late in 1993, males who are not stud quality can be found for $500, sometimes for less. If they have experience as packers, that can add up to a thousand dollars to the price, depending on the amount of experience. If they have stud potential, the price can go up and up, though you can find nice potential studs for as little as $1500, depending on the type of llama you are interested in.

Sound weanling females may be found for as low as $2500, and bred females begin somewhat higher.

These figures are the very lowest I've heard; if you paid $1,000 for a young male to be trained as a packer, $5,000 for a future herd sire, and $4000 for a nice weanling female, those would also be moderate prices. These prices are lower than they were in the late 1980s, but similar to what we paid when we bought our first llamas in 1982.

You can also spend far, far more, if you are interested in moving closer to the top of the market.

Please note that just because you can sometimes find animals for prices this low, not all animals at these (or higher) prices will be sound. One breeder guesstimated to me that some 40% of all llamas had flaws that would make them undesirable as breeding stock. I was surprised at this high a percentage, but whatever the percentage, you can't learn too much about selecting good llamas.

Sometimes if you've done your homework, you can get a good deal because of special circumstances—the seller may be in a hurry to sell for reasons that have nothing to do with llamas.

By the time you are reading this, or in your area of the country, prices may be different. To find out what people are asking, take a look at the classified ads in any of the llama magazines. A lot of the ads don't include prices, but enough do that you can get some idea. Auction prices are public; I particularly recommend *Llama Life's* discussions of auction prices and what they mean.

How do people pay for them?

It's always simplest to pay cash, but people bitten by the llama bug have dreamed up a number of interesting ways to pay for llamas if they didn't happen to have the cash on hand. One determined llama owner, Marcella Hoeltzel, put a $3000 stud on her MasterCard. She did this by getting a cash advance; I have yet to see credit card stickers adorning the display ads of llama ranches.

Chuck and Joanne Forest turned misfortune into llamas. "We bought our first female at auction with money that was an insurance check from a doll collection that was stolen from our house," Chuck told me.

Relatives are a common source of funds, either providing loans or going in on a family business.

We put a second mortgage on our place, which I would only recommend if you have other income from which you can repay the loan. Even then, the added interest might reduce your profits too much. Some other people have used mortgages, while a few have persuaded their bankers to use the llamas as the collateral for loans.

Selling your llamas

Selling llamas is much easier for the well-established, larger ranches that have built up good reputations than it is for smaller or newer ranches. As Fred Bauer cautions, "It's hard to get people to come out and look at one llama, especially if they've never bought any others from you and you don't have a big reputation as a seller."

If you have never sold anything, then selling llamas will be a learning experience. "Llamas sell themselves" used to be a widely repeated comment, and it's true that their great appeal makes them easier to sell than many other items, but it isn't the llamas who decide on the price, make it known they're available, and follow through on the various details.

It's also true that selling llamas is easier in certain times and places than in others. There are market fluctuations, seasonal rhythms, and other factors that come into play. In difficult economic times, you may have llamas that you want to sell but can't easily find buyers for.

In order to get people to come to your place, you will have to promote. Cooperative regional efforts are a great way to attract local people who are just learning about llamas. Ken Rose of Idaho comments, "There are hot lines amongst your regional groups, which I think are very beneficial. If you work within a regional group and see and meet people in your area, and they get to know you and your animals, together you build up a market in your area. If they publish a list of what's for sale in an area, then if you don't have what somebody wants, you show them the list. What goes around, comes around."

Often the llamas affect who buys them. Someone may come to look at a certain animal, and end up falling in love with another one. There's no denying the chemistry that happens between people and llamas at times. As with the chemistry between people, that's not the only condition for a happy relationship but it's nice when it's there.

People who have not sold animals before, especially smaller breeders who spend a lot of time with their llamas, sometimes find it difficult to part with any of their llamas. The main thing that has overcome my sadness has been the happiness of the people buying it. The first time we sold a llama that I particularly loved, I was out in the barn saying goodbye to him (and crying a little) when the people arrived. The parents and children were so thrilled and excited that I easily got caught up in their joy. It was like Christmas, and I was Santa Claus! We have stayed in close touch with some of the people who bought from us. They've become something like cousins by taking our children home with them. Every now and then we get a letter or some baby photos. Then I feel like a grandmother.

Deciding which of your llamas to sell, and when, takes some thinking. You continually have to re-examine your vision of your herd, both present and future. Sometimes that's as simple as a moment's quick thought, but other times your heart may be going in one direction and your mind in another. More than one couple told me that deciding what llamas to sell has been where they've had their greatest disagreements.

Pricing llamas for sale

The type of llama you are selling, its soundness and general appearance, its bloodlines, its level of training, its disposition, and your reputation are all factors in deciding on a price. Some of these factors are more important than others in a particular situation. Sometimes breeders look at one of their animals and consider it only slightly different than one that sold at auction for, say, forty thousand dollars. Does that mean they have a thirty thousand dollar animal, or even a twenty? No. Usually those differences are not really slight. Even if they are, what ranch the llama comes from has a lot to do with what people will pay.

Happy purchasers take home our Whiskers and Levi.

Our pricing has reflected our assessment of the current market, plus sometimes our emotions toward a particular animal. If I've had any doubts about a llama, I've pointed out the situation to the buyer and charged a bit less. One time, we offered a female for sale at a price that was at the higher end of what we guessed she was worth. We felt that if we could get that much for her, the money would be welcome, but we liked her so much ourselves that we wouldn't want to sell her for much less than that. We didn't get it, and we happily kept her.

Once you choose an asking price, decide how firm it is. Many llama shoppers are good bargainers. It's quite common to give a discount if more than one animal is sold at the same time. Ultimately, pricing comes down to what you and someone else can agree on. It's not as though there's a blue book for llamas.

Advertising

The kind of llama you're breeding and the kind of prices you hope to get will help you decide how to advertise. Many breeders find it essential to place color display ads in "the magazine" as *Llamas* is called. They feel this makes an important statement about their presence in the llama market. As there have become more periodicals, there are more places that you can do this. One rule of thumb for this kind of advertising is that repetition is important. Advertising textbooks will tell you that you're better off placing an ad in every issue of a periodical, even if it's a small ad, than to place a more expensive ad rarely.

When you have some animals to sell, then there are specific things you can do. You can get on the phone and tell people what you have. Place a classified ad. The lead time can be fairly long in the llama magazines; the monthly *Llama Link* is probably the fastest. Although many ads don't give prices, again from what I've read about the principles of advertising, classifieds with prices will pull better than those without. You can also place classifieds in agricultural or livestock papers in your region, such as the *Capital Press* in Oregon. You can place a classified in your local paper or super shopper. If you wish, put a sign on your fence, LLAMAS FOR SALE with your phone number; this may yield more casual inquirers and drop-ins, but these people may come back later and buy.

For low-priced males, training adds some dollar value to them, but more importantly it may make the difference between selling and not selling them. It always increases buyer satisfaction and decreases stress to the newly purchased llamas. All llamas should be halter- and lead-trained at the very least.

Once, when we had three females for sale, we did a small mailing to people nearby. Our flyer yielded one sale, our ad in the *Oregonian* another, and a classified in *Llamas* the third. I don't remember how we have connected with all of our various buyers over the years, but one couple took an extension class on llamas that I taught at the local college, and several sales have been to close friends in the llama community. Edie Mattson, who bought the first baby we ever sold, had come to our ranch for a llama day hike.

One Oregon breeder has advertised in llama magazines and in newspapers. "But I know I've sold most of my llamas just through word of mouth and meeting people. I've sold much more that way than through advertising. There's no comparison."

Once you get responses to your ads, some people will want to see color photographs. If you have a video camcorder, I think video can be very helpful, as the amount of information that can be conveyed by video far surpasses what a snapshot will show. Video is especially useful if the potential buyer lives far enough away that a trip will be an inconvenience.

Presenting your llamas

We first met Ken Safley when we bought a llama from him, back in the early 1980s. For this book, I asked his advice about selling llamas. "If you would call me up and say you're going to be here Thursday afternoon, two o'clock, I would be clean-shaven, take a shower, put on clean clothes. I'd meet you, more than likely, out in the driveway at your car. I would bring you into my house and visit somewhat. If you wanted coffee, cake, tea, or whatever, I'd give it to you. And we'd get acquainted and see what you want, and make you feel at home. And then we'd go down and take a look at llamas." I remembered that was exactly what he had done with us.

Ken had further advice. "The most important thing is to know how to present your llamas to your customer. I'll tell you what some people ought to do. They ought to go down in their pasture, look at their llamas, and practice talking out loud. 'And this female is beautiful! Look at the nice colors!' Learn how to present your llamas.

"You have to tell everybody the truth. You don't lie about a thing, but you don't have to mention everything. You don't have to say 'Well, it's got a little head,' or 'Its ears are short,' or 'Well, see how funny its eyes look?' You don't have to mention those things, because how do you know your customer doesn't like them? You let your customer decide whether they want them or not." My style is more forthright, but I can see his point.

Selling at auction

An auction usually offers a concentration of people all intent on buying llamas. Now that there are more choices of auctions, there may be ones that are relatively near you, or ones where the style of the promoters suits you. Breeders may take their best animals to these auctions, as a way of showcasing their ranch. I'm happy to see the greater diversity in auctions.

When I was first selling llamas, I was so attached to my animals that I couldn't have just sold them to whoever spent the most at an auction. So we did the necessary promoting and sold all our babies off the ranch. Today, more small breeders are using auctions.

"If you're going to sell at auction, you should go to one first and price the animals that are there,"Ken Rose said. "Write your prices down, and see if your prices come out close to what the auction prices actually are. Then go home and think about your animal's worth. That way, if you take an animal to an auction, you won't go in expecting too much or not enough."

Before selling at auction, look at what it costs. The commission is as much as 10% of the sale price. Your travel costs, time, motels, meals, and the work of preparing the llama all add up. You can ask a significantly lower price if you sell off your ranch.

Another method of selling animals is through a broker. This is a small part of llama marketing at this time, though it's not uncommon for breeders to buy animals and then resell them.

Love and money in the marketplace

Cutler Umbach told me that the Idaho Breeders Network requires its members to have a clause in their sales agreement along the lines of, "Seller has not concealed any facts, actually known to him, which seller believes would change the buyer's decision to purchase the llama for the price specified."

Cutler explained, "That takes us out of the used car business. I don't like 'buyer beware.' Even though that's the way it is in every other livestock business, I don't think it should be in the llama business. Why not? Because many of the people who are buying llamas have no previous experience with livestock. They can't be expected to have the knowledge not to be taken advantage of and we shouldn't be taking advantage of them."

I liked that. I also like Ken Safley's advice not to impose my personal tastes on other people when they're looking at my llamas. What is fact, which I must tell the buyer, and what is just my opinion, which I may or may not choose to mention? How many of us know how to sort out what is fact and what is opinion in our thinking?

The buying and selling of llamas becomes easier with experience. When you're buying or selling, it can be a challenge to hit the balance point between your love of llamas and your thoughts and feelings about making money with them. When it does all work together, it's very satisfying.

CHAPTER SIX

Promoting and Showing Llamas

ONCE YOU HAVE SOME LLAMAS, many of your friends and acquaintances will be eager to see them—and so will many other people. The opportunities to do things with llamas in your community are unlimited. If you have the time and the inclination, you can offer ranch visits, take llamas on any number of outings, and join together with other people to put on all kinds of llama events. In promoting llamas, the love and money aspects come together very nicely: public relations activities bring pleasure to other people at the same time that they let the world know that you are in the llama business.

Llama shows have become popular. There are many performance events for adults and children, such as obstacle races and showmanship. There are also halter classes, in which the animals are judged on their appearance.

Visitors

"Dorrie's barking again. It looks there's like a car coming up the driveway," was a frequent comment at our ranch. We lived a mile off a major freeway, on a road leading to a ski resort, so there was a fair amount of traffic. Sometimes people followed their impulse to drop in.

One of us would go out and conduct a llama tour. We generally enjoyed these breaks in our routine, and on days when we were too busy or just felt like being alone, we simply closed the gate across our driveway, as we did when we went to town. We put a PRIVATE sign down by the road, rather than a NO TRESPASSING one, to be a little friendlier.

I've heard it said many times that you should make your place beautiful to enhance the look of the llamas. One or two old rusted vehicles with flat tires, and the kind of clutter that working ranches often accumulate, could affect buyers adversely, especially if the llamas were upscale in price. But beyond cleaning up the obvious messes, I think how much work you put into beautifying your place is a matter of personal style and situation. It's more important how the llamas are treated than whether the place is a showpiece.

If you enjoy having visitors, there are many groups in your community that would love to be invited. Church groups, school classes, senior citizen groups: the list is endless.

Cutler and Nancy Umbach own llamas in a resort town. "Tourists come and want to see what it's all about, often without any real desire to own llamas," Cutler told me. "So we set up a deal where they come nine o'clock on occasional Saturday mornings for an hour's tour. Potential purchasers are a different story. If someone calls up and says, 'I'm interested in buying llamas,' we are available."

There's a lot of public education involved. After I'd been asked, "Don't they spit?" dozens of times, I developed several replies. "Yes, but wouldn't you rather be spat on than kicked or bitten?" was my briefest one. Sometimes I explained that spitting is part of the llamas' system of communicating with each other. Typically they first give other signals of annoyance, such as putting their ears back and raising their heads. Then, if the other llama doesn't get the message, they may spit. I've been spat upon when two llamas were disputing who would have a particular position at the hay rack I was filling. One llama spat—as they often do—off to the side of the other one, just as I wandered into the wrong place at the wrong time!

There are some informative brochures put out by llama associations which you can keep on hand for visitors.

Many people can't or don't want to take the time to visit with everyone who's curious about llamas. Just because you bought a couple of animals doesn't mean you opened a zoo. One busy breeder with a large number of animals told me, "If people want to come and see the llamas and are not ever thinking of buying, they may not tell you that on the phone. But when they are here, I can figure it out. Then pretty soon I just start walking to the front gate. People tend to follow you to their car!"

Linda Rodgers holds a visitor up to meet Twister.

If you're having visitors, it would be prudent to check your ranch or farm liability insurance policy, and see that it covers people stopping by to visit livestock.

Llama outings

Want to draw a crowd? Just go somewhere with some llamas. Stick your business cards in your pocket, and have fun! The sidebar includes a lot of enjoyable things to do, and there are many more.

Any llamas that are going to be out in public should be well suited for it. Once I took Poco, my favorite public relations llama, to a festival held in a city park. It was a lovely day, and there were a lot of people there. Poco and I strolled around, chatting with people, and I handed out flyers describing our llama hikes. At one point, Poco had five lively teenagers gathered around his head, petting him and joking around with each other, when a grandmother and two preschoolers clustered around his rear. The little ones pushed their hands into his back legs and tugged on his wool. Poco was quite content, but I soon got the people away from his rear. Some of my other llamas would not have been as reliable when crowded, and for that reason, I would not have taken them to the park. It often surprises me how casual the general public can be about standing directly behind the rear legs of

LOCAL P.R. SUGGESTIONS

*Parades: Fourth of July, etc. Llamas adjust well to the cheers of crowds. They are crowd stoppers so be prepared to stay awhile and answer lots of questions afterward.

*Visit a nursery school with a llama.

*Jog with your llama.

*Visit a park with your llama.

*Take a walk on the beach.

*Hike a trail.

*Stroll a city street.

*Park your rig in a shopping center parking lot with a llama peeking out.

*Find and enter a pet contest—you're sure to win in some category.

*Volunteer your llama to visit convalescent homes for children or for adults, with groups like "Tender Loving Zoo."

*Offer to visit cancer groups like "Make Today Count" and "Ronald McDonald House."

*Offer your llamas for a fund raiser: photo buttons of children hugging your llama, set up a petting corral, etc.

*Offer a gourmet llama hike for the afternoon as an item in a local fund raising auction.

*Use llamas in animal education classes in summer schools, public animal shelters, private animal care center programs, and youth center programs.

*Contact your local outfitter for hiking and sporting equipment. He can use a llama for promotion and you can use the exposure.

*Make yourself available for interviews for human interest stories in your local magazines, newspapers, radio, and TV.

*Take advantage of radio talk shows during open forum hours, or use llamas as an example of animals relieving stress on one of the popular psychology talk shows.

*Llamas are attention-getters for political campaigns.

*Boy Scouts, Girl Scouts, Brownies, Campfire, and 4-H can use llamas for leadership and other project experience.

*Llamas can attract the public to other businesses, lodges, parks, bed and breakfasts, etc.

*They can carry Christmas trees out of Christmas tree forests.

* Llamas pack out grapes, apples, and other fruit from the fields.

*Llamas work well in programs for blind, deaf, disturbed, and other children.

*Offer some of your llama wool free to your local spinners and weavers guild to promote good will and eventually to create a good market for your wool.

*Offer llamas for a children's summer camp experience.

*Llamas are a hit as invited guests at children's birthday and holiday parties.

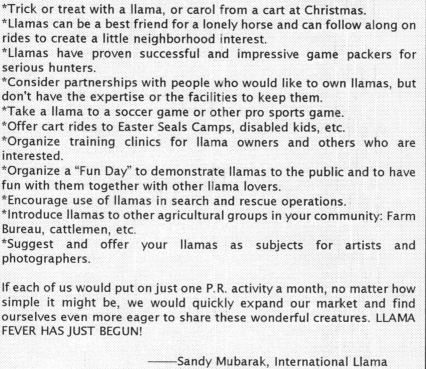

*Trick or treat with a llama, or carol from a cart at Christmas.
*Llamas can be a best friend for a lonely horse and can follow along on rides to create a little neighborhood interest.
*Llamas have proven successful and impressive game packers for serious hunters.
*Consider partnerships with people who would like to own llamas, but don't have the expertise or the facilities to keep them.
*Take a llama to a soccer game or other pro sports game.
*Offer cart rides to Easter Seals Camps, disabled kids, etc.
*Organize training clinics for llama owners and others who are interested.
*Organize a "Fun Day" to demonstrate llamas to the public and to have fun with them together with other llama lovers.
*Encourage use of llamas in search and rescue operations.
*Introduce llamas to other agricultural groups in your community: Farm Bureau, cattlemen, etc.
*Suggest and offer your llamas as subjects for artists and photographers.

If each of us would put on just one P.R. activity a month, no matter how simple it might be, we would quickly expand our market and find ourselves even more eager to share these wonderful creatures. LLAMA FEVER HAS JUST BEGUN!

————Sandy Mubarak, International Llama Association P.R. Committee

a llama. Do they do the same thing with horses and mules?

What makes a good PR llama? I prefer the ones with steadier dispositions to start with. Then training makes a great deal of difference. A method of training called TTEAM is particularly suited to helping llamas become more comfortable with being touched. Llamas don't crave petting, the way most dogs and cats do, but many of them acquire a taste or at least a tolerance for it.

Cathy Crisman is a llama owner in Washington who has taken her animals to nursing homes for a number of years. She comments, "Ideally, the llama used in pet therapy is docile, inquisitive, hums at times, does not kick, can be touched on body and neck without reprisal, and enjoys new experiences." Sounds like a great llama for any purpose!

Poco always announced when he'd had enough PR work. When he began to tire at an event, he hummed more and more insistently. It wouldn't take long for us to understand his message.

Local publicity

It's no longer news fit for the newspaper or television that you've come home with some llamas, but it may not take much more of an event than that to interest the media. When we applied for a permit from the county to operate a llama hikes business on our ranch, the coverage we received was quite a nice boost to starting the hikes.

Not all of it was exactly what we wanted. The front page story in one paper headlined, "Wanna llama? Better pack a bundle of bucks; the craze is getting spendy." That article was riddled with inaccuracies. But most reporters are more careful.

When we took Thundercloud to the bank to get the cover photograph for this book, we had of course made advance arrangements with the bank manager. She, or someone in the bank, had told the local paper, as a reporter/photographer was on hand. The paper ran a very nice front-page piece with a picture of Thundercloud in the bank, under the headline "Now that's full-service banking."

If the media don't come seeking you out, you can phone them with news of an event such as the arrival of a photogenic baby llama. Or a press release can generate some interest. Press releases are typically short—one page is better than two—and double-spaced. There should be a box in the upper right-hand corner that looks something like this:

FOR IMMEDIATE RELEASE
CONTACT: Your Name(s)
Phone number(s)

If you have different day and evening phones, you might list them both, indicating which is which. You want to make it as easy as possible for someone to reach you, not just your machine.

Next comes a short headline and then the article. Don't let uncertainty about your writing ability keep you from doing a press release, but if it is interestingly written, often the newspapers or magazines will simply run much of it as is. Write it so that the most important points are at the beginning, in case it gets shortened. If you go over one page, on the bottom line of the first page, centered, put

-more-

and at the end of the press release, put

-end-

If you have any well focussed, high-contrast black and white photos, they can accompany the press release. They should not be screened.

Llama owners promote llamas together

While some very energetic llama owners have put on public events by themselves, many others have naturally gotten together to take on large projects: from group llama displays at a county fair to major national gatherings. Llamas go to the National Western Stock Show in Denver and to many state and county fairs. There is a lot of work behind an event like that—and also a lot of satisfaction, seeing how much interest there is in llamas. The Oklahoma State Fair chose the theme "Lights, Laughs, and Llamas" one year, using a llama in its logo. There had been llamas at the fair for a few years, with a good public response.

In central Oregon, where there are many llama ranches, Nancy Chlarson of Quality Llama Products spearheaded an annual "Central Oregon Llama Tour and Farm Visit Day" every summer, usually late in August. Llama people from all over, as well as people from the region (which could be called the llama capital of the US) spend the Saturday going to several ranches in tour busses. As well as seeing the llamas and the ranches, the guests hear informative presentations and receive a catalog with articles, maps, and ads. That evening, there is a dinner and entertainment, sometimes with a slide show of all the ranches that will be holding open house on Sunday. People visit and often buy llamas at the ranches on the Sunday. Llamas, information, and entertainment—a great combination!

Llama breeders that live near each other often put together a brochure, listing the farms with a few appealing llama photographs, farm phone numbers, and a general map. Sometimes a section of llama information is included. One brochure I received, from the Yosemite Llama Breeders, described an annual open house much like the Central Oregon one, and included a separate page listing the animals for sale at the various ranches. A number of groups, such as the Idaho breeders network, have advertised in the llama periodicals as well as to the general public.

Other groups have put on one-day informational events, either veterinary or general. They have put on stud service auctions. In Colorado, a lot of llama labor (and llama-owner labor) went into trail creation with the Colorado Trail Project.

Promoting llamas within the llama community

One of the reasons that people promote their llamas is to become known by other llama owners. This happens if you take part in llama events. Many people take photo albums of their animals along with them to llama gatherings, whether or not they bring their animals. This can be a low-cost way of showing your herd to interested people. (But be sensitive to just how interested they are! I have several times been in the clutches of someone going on and on about their animals, oblivious that my interest had worn thin.) Also, at many gatherings, you can reserve a booth.

Another way to become known is to place display advertisements, either color or black and white, in the magazines. What factors influence when such an ad is a good decision? Certainly for anyone with a large herd or with studs they are promoting, it's a way to become known. For breeders with just a handful of animals who utilize their own non-flashy males, it's probably not important. For the many breeders who fall in between these extremes, it's a matter of personal style and budget. Several breeders I spoke with said they didn't know how to gauge the results of their ads, but they felt that it was important to place them.

One serious breeder of moderately priced animals cautioned, "The top of the line animals are largely a matter of promotion. There is a fictitious elitism—well, it exists in people's minds so it's real—so the more highly promoted farms maintain higher prices because they can make you think they are worth it. That's what advertising is about, anyway!"

She added that if you try to get into this league, and it isn't really natural to you, it could be a big mistake. It's important to think about who you are and where your market base is, in doing your advertising as in setting your prices.

Llama shows

Halter classes—that is, classes where judging is based largely on the appearance of the llamas—are gaining popularity but also have their critics in the llama world. Since there are no agreed-upon breed standards yet, how can judging be otherwise than subjective?

One group that has worked very hard to tackle these questions is ALSA, formerly the American Llama Show Association and now the Alpaca and Llama Show Association. They have come up with guidelines for judging. These guidelines are derived from a list of negative llama traits compiled by two foremost llama veterinary researchers—Murray E. Fowler, DVM, and LaRue W. Johnson, DVM. A list of positive characteristics was also developed. These lists have been modified for use with alpacas as well.

Jodi Sleeper explained how judging works. "Using the positive and negative traits as his basis, the judge compares the llamas to each other and places them according to this comparison. This system of judging is termed a relative system as opposed to judging to a specific breed standard. Those people who argue that we do not have specific standards for llamas, and therefore have no criteria for judging, seem to be overlooking the immense amount of information that we do have.

"The lists of traits developed by ALSA do not describe specifically the ideal llama but they do take advantage of what the experts tell us is a sound and healthy llama. We do not need to say how tall or how heavy because we know there is a wide and maybe natural variance."

ALSA judge (and trainer of judges) Lynn Hyder told me that soundness must be the judge's first consideration. Next comes conformation, and next disposition. Hyder says that he refers his students to Dr. Murray E. Fowler's classic *Llamas* article, "Form, Function, Conformation, and Soundness."

ALSA has a point system. To become a champion, a llama must earn a total of thirty-five points from at least four shows, and under at least five judges. A minimum of ten points must be in halter classes, and a minimum of fifteen must be in performance classes, where judging is based on what the llamas and people do. I like this emphasis much better than what I see, for example, at AKC dog shows, where obedience is just a tiny part of things.

From the Alpaca and Llama Show Association:
Soundness, Conformation, and Disposition
Desirable for Breeding Llamas
(Excerpted from the ALSA handbook in their 1990 magazine of shows and information. © 1990, ALSA. Used by permission.)

The Halter Class Division is designed to judge llamas on their healthy breeding qualities. The following list of positive and negative traits has been developed as a judging criteria for soundness, conformation, and disposition in breeding quality llamas.

ALSA defines soundness as free from flaw, defect, disease, or injury. Further, ALSA defines unsoundness as physical disability that diminishes the function of a part of the body. In judging animals, the potential for unsoundness depends on the use or purpose of the animal.

ALSA defines conformation as the appropriate arrangement of body parts for assembly into the whole animal. Overall balance is considered to be a component of conformation and may be defined as the proportionate shape or contour of the animal.

POSITIVE TRAITS

A. *Overall Appearance*: The llama should be well proportioned, balanced, and symmetrical.

B. *Head*: The head should be carried proudly and alertly. The jaw formation should exhibit correct bite and dentition.

C. *Front Legs*: The front legs should be relatively straight with generally forward facing toes and properly angled pasterns. There should be good bone density.

D. *Rear Legs*: The rear legs should be relatively straight from hock to fetlock joint when viewed from the side or rear. The toes should be generally forward facing and the pasterns should be properly angled. There should be good bone density.

E. *Movement*: All limbs should move freely and smoothly.

F. *Fiber*: The fiber should have a healthy luster.

G. *Reproductive Organs*: The testicles should both be visible and appear uniform. Female genitalia should be normal appearing.

H. *Disposition*: A good disposition is highly desirable.

NEGATIVE TRAITS

A. *Angular Limb Deformity*: Excessive lateral or medial deviation of the bones and joints of the front and rear legs.

B. *Humped back*: An increased convexity or upward curvature of the top line of the back.

C. *Sway back*: An increased concavity or downward curvature of the top line of the back.

D. *Post-leggedness*: Essentially a straight line from the stifle to the fetlock without the normal zig zag pattern of the hind leg.

E. *Dropped fetlock or pastern*: A weak pastern or less than normal angle of the pastern possibly resulting in the fetlock and/or pastern touching the ground.

F. *Cow hocked*: As viewed from behind, the hocks are excessively deviated towards the midline.

G. *Sickle-hocked*: As viewed from the side, there is marked hock flexion resulting in the hind cannon bone being at an angle instead of nearly vertical.

H. *Ectopic Testicles*: One or both testicles not found in their usual location.

I. *Jaw Malocclusions*: Either the upper jaw is too short or the lower jaw is too long, resulting in protruding lower teeth. Occasionally the lower jaw is too short or the upper jaw is too long.

J. *Female External Genitalia Abnormalities*: This includes vaginal shelving (lips of the vulva approaching horizontal plane instead of normal near vertical plane), a tipped up tip of the vulva, a very small vulva, or the presence of prominent clitoris (consistent with hermaphroditism).

K. *Umbilical Hernia*: The presence of a soft fluctuant bulge at the site of the umbilicus.

L. *Gopher Ears*: Short, stubby ears that are not due to frostbite but are rather congenital and hereditary.

M. *Gonadal Hypoplasia*: Smallness of either one or both testicles.

N. *History of the Surgical Correction for:* Angular Limb Deformity, Shortening of the jaw, Hernia, Choanel Atresia, Hermaphroditism, Ectopic testicles.

"I'm a real advocate of llama shows," Averill Abbott told me. "What I am really trying to promote is the obstacle course, PR llama, pack races, all those fun things. And showmanship. I really push showmanship because anybody can take any llama and do it. There you're being judged on how well you show that llama, and it has nothing to do with that llama's conformation. A better trained llama is a better shown llama, so training is emphasized.

"It's fun to go to shows. You get to socialize with other llama people. I enjoy the atmosphere. People love it if they have something to do when they go to a show. They don't have to have an offspring of some big name animal. They can have anything. It's great for the kids—llamas are so easy to handle—and the llamas like it too! I really hope shows expand."

Another breeder, Heather Bamford, told me, "I show my animals as a form of advertising. I don't do it to win ribbons, or to compete. It really pays off for us. We get more inquiries from showing and displays than we do from magazine ads. Because we're small and out of the way, we bring our llamas to the shows, where the people are."

Grooming for shows

If you are entering a llama in a halter class at a show, grooming preparations can be quite time-consuming. Some people begin grooming by using a blower. For packing, a regular leaf blower is adequate, but there are also commercial heavy-duty blowers which deliver a lot more air, and—a nice touch—it can be warm. After the initial surprise, most llamas quite like the blowing, and lean into the current of air. A lot of dust and small debris comes out this way, and it opens up the coat a bit. Be aware, though, that one of the heavy-duty blowers can tangle long wool.

A few last-minute touches

For the combing process, different kinds of tools are used. Llamas will differ in how long they are willing to let you comb them out at one time. Especially at first, several short sessions a day, or a longer session which includes several breaks for snacks and maybe a stroll, are far better than trying to do a long unrelenting session. Remember, you acquired llamas to have fun with them! Don't plan on combing out a long-wooled llama in just one day. It can take quite a few days if the wool is very long or matted. If you are impatient, the llama is likely to be tense as well.

Shampooing a llama is something I've never attempted. You might want to if you were competing in halter classes, taking a llama to sell at an auction, or simply wanted the animal to look gorgeous for promotional photographs or at an event. Otherwise, the llamas can live their whole lives through without needing this kind of cleaning. Llama owners who've done it tell me that it takes a good part of a day, by the time you wash (don't rub, as you don't want the wool matted), rinse, and blow-dry. You must have already groomed the llama thoroughly before the shampoo. At the end of all this, cover your llama with a llama blanket or something you've designed to fit around the animal. You don't want one quick roll in the dust to destroy the effect!

Pros and cons of shows

I love performance events at shows. I'm often in awe at the closeness of the cooperation between llama and human. Llama owners in the audience roar with laughter when a llama pulls back and refuses to go under a clothesline or over a bridge. We've been there ourselves, in our own fields or on the trail, and it's endearing to watch the people and llamas working things out in public. My heart fills up when a llama's trust of its handler overcomes its fear of a spooky obstacle.

But halter classes are not my cup of tea. Francie Greth-Peto said, "In any one collection of llamas amassed before a judge in a halter class, there will be one animal that is selected out as the best, a couple more will 'place,' and all the other beautiful, gentle, well-behaved, and lovely animals will leave the arena as also-rans, as less valuable in the eyes of many than they were just an hour before."

Francie says that sometimes when she expresses her dislike of shows, someone will say to her. "It's just for fun." Her response is to ask, "If it is truly just for fun, then why do you need rewards such as ribbons and points?" This helped me see that my lack of ease with halter classes reflects my dislike for our society's emphasis on competition and winning.

Some breeders worry that in order to be recognized in the market, they would have to take part in what is often called a 'trailer race,' where you simply have to spend thousands of dollars and travel thousands of miles to enter shows. And you'd better win some, too. This may happen to an extent with llamas, but many breeders don't play the game that way.

Another reason not to compete in halter class is that you may be able to promote more effectively by not entering it. Suppose that you have a magnificent stud, one that might well take first place. Some owners have brought such animals to events but not entered them in the competition, thinking that it wasn't worth risking taking second place—or worse. They preferred to let people form their own opinions about the animal by seeing it. An interesting strategy.

CHAPTER SEVEN:

Alpacas

THE ALPACA INDUSTRY is very new in North America. As recently as 1983, some zoos and a handful of individuals owned a few of these diminutive relatives of the llama. Then hundreds of alpacas were imported from South America. Now, people are eagerly buying alpacas, with females selling from about $12,500 to over $30,000 and stud-quality males beginning around $7,500. Even pet quality males command considerably higher prices than equivalent llamas. There are a few thousand alpacas here now. Demand is greater than supply, and seems likely to remain so for some time.

Why are alpacas so appealing?

Both love and money. The alpacas are charming, and the profitability per animal is greater than for llamas.

Many alpaca owners began with llamas, and may indeed still have llamas. But somewhere along the line, they were introduced to alpacas, and they fell in love. They describe their little alpacas (weighing one-third to one-half what a llama weighs) as much easier to manage, and with charming personalities, not unlike llamas but with endearing characteristics of their own. Dr. Ralph Uber told me, "Alpacas are more personable. They aren't as apprehensive. I do love llamas, and I have some llamas that I would never part with. But in general all the alpacas are gentle, where some of the llamas are more distant and more spooky."

Cecile Champagne comments, "Everybody knows how easy llamas are to take care of, and alpacas are probably six times easier. They eat less than half as much as a llama. They poop about a sixth as much as a llama. They're so easy to manage.

"When the vet comes into a llama pen, the llamas take off to the four corners. He comes into an alpaca pen, and they all herd together behind the dominant alpaca. This is another way they are easier to work with. You've got the whole bunch there together.

"Their flockiness helps when I move them around. Our pens don't have grass in them, but we've got a lot of grass outside the pens.

Alpacas are smaller and woollier than llamas.

So I let some out every day to eat the grass, and then when it's time to go back in I just walk behind them and shoo them, and they all go back in.

"The only time I think it would be a disadvantage is if a bad dog came into the pen. Where llamas might take after that dog, few alpacas would challenge a dog. I think they'd all get into their little flock.

"When we had just the llamas, as they were growing up, they would reach a certain size and I would always wish they'd stay that size; they were so wonderful, lovable, cute. That's what I love about the alpacas; they stay there. And they have these darling miniature babies."

The income potential is primarily in the breeding, with the wool as the primary end-use. The pet aspect is likely to grow as a factor; any alpacas who turn out to be not suitable for breeding stock will no doubt be greatly loved as pets and for their wool.

In South America, there are over three million alpacas, mostly in Peru, with some herds numbering as many as sixty thousand. In one year recently, Peru exported over three thousand tons of alpaca wool, valued at $24 million US. Over thousands of years, the alpaca has been selectively bred for wool by the Indians of South America. Alpaca wool is typically denser, finer, and softer than llama wool. Where llama wool may have coarse guard hairs in it, alpaca wool for the most part doesn't.

Breeders in North America, as well as in New Zealand and Australia, where wool is already big business, are excited about the long-range potential of the alpaca industry in their own regions. I spoke with several alpaca breeders who were enjoying the sense of being in on the very beginning of a new industry. "They're about where the llamas were twelve years ago," Ken Safley told me. Dr. Uber, one of the few people to have alpacas before the importation, commented, "We feel that there's going to be a big explosion, as far as the alpaca market is concerned, in the next few years. The interest has really increased. There are more inquiries than ever before. It looks like a very good future for the industry."

Because alpaca prices are higher and costs are lower than for llamas, it appears that there is a much higher profit margin for alpacas than for llamas. The Alpaca Owners and Breeders Association (AOBA, listed in the Resource Guide) puts out a little booklet,

"Alpacas: The world's finest livestock investment," which is nicely done and very persuasive. It includes spreadsheets which show a very handsome profit; I'd encourage anyone thinking about llamas or alpacas as an investment to take a good look at alpacas.

I do have a concern about the spreadsheet: it shows a return on investment based on keeping your entire herd for ten years, which could crowd your facilities, as with their assumptions, you would start with 11 animals and end up with 132! Such a strategy could also backfire if prices fell near the end of the ten years; they do discuss price sensitivity in the booklet. See my discussion of spreadsheets in chapter 10 of this book. Still, if I were buying llamas or alpacas for their investment value, it would probably be alpacas.

The Wool

In South America, two breeds of alpacas are recognized, depending on the wool: the huacaya and the suri, with the suri having the longer, silkier wool. When the two breeds are crossed, the first generation will be all huacaya in appearance, but it will carry genes for both types. The second generations will be divided between the two breeds. Once in a while, parents of one breed will produce a baby of the other. In Peru, the huacaya account for about ninety percent of the animals, and in this country they constitute closer to ninety-nine percent.

Alpaca wool is soft, surpassed only by the wool of its distant (and wild) relative, the vicuna. It has a uniform fineness. It may have a lot of crimp in the wool—the equivalent, roughly, of naturally curly hair on a human—or it may not. Crimp is favored in judging. Alpaca wool is about three times stronger than sheep's wool, which is thicker.

White is commercially the most valuable color in South America, since it can be dyed. Here, it is also popular, but many spinners seek out the other rich colors alpacas come in: brown, caramel, gray, black, and some other lovely shades such as rose-gray and rust. Unlike llamas, alpacas most often come in solid colors, a plus for using their wool.

In this country, handspinners are at present the primary market for alpaca fleece. Some alpaca owners shear their animals every two years. using electric shears or hand shears, doing it themselves or hiring a sheep shearer. They may get around eight pounds of wool per alpaca; one owner reports selling half-fleeces at around $200 each. That adds up to more profit in wool than llamas yield, which is as it

should be after six thousand years of selective breeding. Alpaca wool requires less preparation before marketing than llama wool.

"In my experience, most alpaca owners tend to shear annually," commented Nard Mullan. "The fleece is better quality—less weathered—and it's better for the health of the animals. They won't overheat. Since alpacas don't shed like llamas, overheating is a concern."

Care and breeding

Most details of care are very similar to llamas. Alpacas eat about a third as much. They require similar fencing, for dog protection. Transporting alpacas is even easier than transporting llamas, because of their smaller size. One breeder hauls four alpacas at a time in his VW van.

Alpacas' front teeth can grow too long, but they can be sawed or filed down and smoothed off by owners with little or no trauma to the animals. Veterinary obstetrical wire may be used for this process. One reason that alpacas are believed to be descended, over many thousands of years, from vicunas, while llamas are descended from guanacos, is the difference in dentition between alpacas and llamas. Llamas' front teeth don't continue to grow in the same way. In addition, in both vicunas and alpacas, the back sides of the teeth lack enamel.

"So far, to me, this is the most challenging aspect of alpaca breeding," Dennis Mullan told me. He and his wife, Nard, are beginning their herd with an adult pair of alpacas. They have already had one adorable baby. Nard added, "I've even seen one breeder use a special grinding bit on his electric drill to grind down front teeth."

While alpacas average around 130 pounds in weight, there are some larger ones. Dr. Uber has a herd of 'English' alpacas, which he bought from the Patterson ranch. These animals are descended from some which lived in England for a few generations, and they are much larger than most other alpacas. Their improved diet may be a factor, but it could also be genetic. Dr. Uber comments, "I've been in Peru, and I saw big alpacas there. And there are some big ones in the U.S. that came from Chile. But the majority of the Chilean imports that I've seen have been under 160 pounds."

As I read through issues of *Alpacas!*, much regarding breeding reminded me of llamas. Alpaca babies are smaller than llama ones, and the mothers may carry them for about two weeks less on the average.

Where South American alpacas have a fertility rate in the forty to fifty percent rate, North American ones, receiving better nutrition and individual attention, have a far, far higher rate.

Cecile Champagne comments, "Birthing seems to be easier for the alpacas than for the llamas. I always know when the llamas are going to give birth that day. At first I couldn't read the alpacas. They'd be eating and chewing their cud and acting perfectly normal, and I'd go in the house. Fifteen minutes later, there would be a baby.

"They have bigger babies for their size. Our alpacas only weigh about 120 pounds, but the babies have ranged between ten and eighteen pounds. They've been wonderful mothers. We haven't had one that wasn't a good mother and a good nurser. Out of over sixty births, we've had just one birth problem."

Training and temperament

At an International Llama Association Jamboree, one alpaca was entered with twenty-nine llamas in the competition for "top public relations llama." The animals had to climb stairs as they might have to do in going to hospitals or schools, go through a noisy grandstand, and be petted by strangers. The alpaca won.

Training is much like llama training, though a bit easier because of the smaller size, more docile nature, and greater tendency to give in. Cecile Champagne suggests that a dog harness can be put on a weanling alpaca, as a tool for controlling the first leading lessons. Once the youngster gets the hang of leading, just an ordinary halter suffices.

She adds, "They seem like they're smarter than llamas in a way because I can teach them to lead so much faster than the llama. It's easier for me and they just don't fight as much. These were almost four-year-old ladies I trained. If I took a four-year-old lady llama that had never been haltered, and tried to train her in two fifteen-minute sessions I don't think I would be terribly successful."

Alpacas are more inclined to kick than are llamas, so some owners work on desensitizing their alpacas' back legs. The 'berserk male syndrome' which occurs rarely in llamas has also been reported in a very small number of alpacas.

Alpacas seem to like water more than llamas do. They like to walk in it, to cool off in it, and to eat plants from marshy areas, which indeed their forebears did around Lake Titicaca in Peru. Several alpaca owners have commented that alpacas are more apt to stay out in the rain than are llamas.

Interbreeding alpacas and llamas: not advised

Since llamas and alpacas are such close relatives that interbreeding is possible between the two species and since the woolly look is popular in llamas, there could be something of a temptation to interbreed. Indeed, many of the llamas imported from South America and sold for high prices may have alpaca somewhere in their parentage.

Perhaps because there are now so many woolly llama studs, there seems to be very little interbreeding going on in North America. Most breeders recognize that the two species are different, and deserve to be kept distinct. As Dr. Uber puts it, "You wouldn't cross a bulldog with a dingo."

What's desirable in conformation is different in the two species. In alpacas, desirable traits include a rounded back, a lower tail set than in llamas, and smaller, more pointed ears.

Alpaca owners are ahead of the llama community in their commitment to keeping their animals pure. Blood typing is a key tool in their efforts. Relatively new for both llamas and alpacas, blood typing identifies genetic markers in the blood, and is useful in solving cases of uncertain parentage and in other ways. The Alpaca Registry, presently run under the ILR or International Lama Registry, requires blood typing. There are alpacas in the registry, from Canada, Australia, England, and Japan as well as the US. The registry is closed, which means that animals to be entered must be offspring of the initial registered stock (and have compatible blood to their believed parents) or they have to apply to a screening committee of the Alpaca Owners and Breeders Association, which has specific guidelines.

Buying alpacas

If you become interested in buying alpacas, be sure that any animals being sold as alpacas are registered with the Alpaca Registry of the ILR. The certificate must bear a gold embossed seal verifying that the alpaca was blood typed.

It's fun to be in on the start of an exciting venture with a vast potential. When that venture gives you the opportunity to spend time with endearing, delightful animals, what could be nicer? The alpaca owners that I've talked to are greatly enjoying themselves.

CHAPTER EIGHT:

Commercial Llama Packing

COMMERCIAL LLAMA PACKING IS A DREAM for many llama owners. After all, what could be more fun than doing something you love, with animals you love and friendly people—and getting paid for it?

And what better life for the llamas? They've been packing for thousands of years. They've been bred for it, they've done it all over the Andes, they are good at it, and they love it. Bobra Goldsmith comments that when she first puts a pack on a young llama she's training, he may be surprised for a little while, but very soon he settles down and responds as if he's saying, "Oh yes, I was born for this." Jay Rais has said in *Llamas*, "First and foremost, llamas are PACK animals. I feel sorry for the poor pen-raised 'show' llamas who will never experience a mountain vista or a sunrise in the Sawtooths."

Francie Greth-Peto and Guy Peto of Mama's Llamas were among the very first people to do commercial llama packing in North America. Guy had been an attorney and in the late 1970s was looking for a career change. "He wanted to have a business where he would encounter people in a positive part of their lives, when they were having fun," Francie said. "He had a lot of backpacking experience, and I had enough that we felt comfortable taking people out into the backcountry. And we thought, why not do it with llamas? If the South American Indians can take their llamas anywhere they go, carrying loads, why not us? That's really where it started, in making the people's journey more comfortable by not having to carry packs, and more interesting by having llamas."

Those people who have made their packing businesses successful all speak of the satisfaction they feel from creating a situation where their guests have a good wilderness experience, enhanced by the llamas. Tom Landis of Oregon Llamas commented, "One of the most fulfilling things for me is watching the llamas and the people interact. It's kind of fun to look at the people beforehand, and try to figure out which llama they're going to become attached to. Most of the people are from cities and are never going to have llamas themselves."

Every commercial packer I've ever spoken to has said that running a commercial pack business takes an immense amount of work. It calls for a variety of skills falling into four main categories: work with the llamas, of course; dealing with the government bureaucracies where you want to hike; marketing the trips; and pleasing your customers, which involves both good organizational skills and the ability to manage and interact with people in the backcountry. In this chapter, I'll discuss each of these, as well as finances, day hikes, and the future of llama packing.

Selecting llamas for packing

"The knowledge and the love of the animals is where you have to start, because you have to have a good working relationship with your animals. You have to enjoy them, you have to know how to take care of them," said Francie Greth-Peto. "But I don't think the love of the animals is enough to be a packer. Initially I was star-struck and I thought it would be. In reality, that's a minor, minor part of a commercial pack business."

In selecting llamas for packing, be very particular about the conformation of the animals. Just as not all llamas are suitable for breeding, not all llamas are going to be good packers. People differ in their preferences, but what is essential is that the animal's build is such that he will be able to walk and carry weight mile after mile. Sound legs are important here. Notice how the llama walks.

Most packers prefer short wool. As Russ Shields of Pack-a-Llama puts it, "For packing, the woolly llamas are no good. Every burr gets into them. You get them on a hot trail, they overheat. For packing, I prefer short hair. It's easy to brush and groom and get going. I use a blower on my packers, maybe five minutes on each one before we leave home. Then in the backcountry, I use a dog slicker brush to go over where the packs and cinches are going, to be sure there are no burrs or anything in the way. When I take my one woolly llama on the trail, it usually takes me half an hour or forty-five minutes every day to get him groomed." Many people who have woolly llamas shear the animals.

Temperament and training are crucial in llamas for a pack string. Most of the people the llamas will be hiking with won't know the first thing about llamas; they may have no animal experience at all. They will be of all ages and levels of fitness. There are some llamas that just don't have the personality for the work. And any llama, no matter how gentle and tranquil, will benefit from practice hiking before he goes out on a commercial trip.

Government bureaucracy

Selecting where to do a packing business is one of the early steps in considering the business, because in order to do commercial packing on public land, you have to get a permit from the agency that administers the land. It can take months or even years, and it isn't automatically granted. "If somebody asked me if they should start a llama packing business, I would tell them they're crazy!" said Russ Shields. "The reason I say that is there's a lot of hard work getting started. In California, you have to have over half a million dollars' worth of insurance; the parks require it. They have limited the backcountry use so that they only allow so many outfitters and guides in each area. In order to get in today, you have to prove need and prove that existing horse and mule packers and guides are not providing this need. So in some parts of the country it's impossible.

"Until you learn how to work the bureaucracy, the answer from the parks is automatically no. But there are certain ways. Most of the llama packers will be more than willing to help. When I first got started, Stephen Biggs and Francie Greth-Peto were very helpful. I told them I was going into competition with them, I was having trouble with this and that, and they sat down and told me what I was getting into." Stephen Biggs of Shasta Llamas started packing in the late 1970s, about the same time as Francie and Guy did.

Marketing

"If I were talking to somebody who wanted to start a llama packing business," said Tom Landis, "I'd say before they worry about llamas, equipment, or anything, to worry about their market. If they don't have any customers, they don't have a business.

"You've got to promote, and promote hard, and start early. I've advertised in many outdoor magazines. I've gone in parades and trade shows. One of the most effective ways of promoting is to pursue free advertising: TV shows, radio shows, magazine articles, newspaper articles. You can pursue those and if you work hard, you can get quite a bit of ink. I think that's a very effective way of getting yourself known.

"But truthfully, it's my big groups that have been my bread and butter." Oregon Llamas has organized trips for the Sierra Club, the Stanford University Travel Study Program, and other groups.

Tom continued, "In the first years, even with the efforts I put into advertising and things like that, I wasn't able to drum up as much business as I could have used. Now at least half of the business that I've got booked is returns and referrals, which is gratifying. I hate

This llama eagerly follows Tom Landis (and food).

promoting and advertising. You have to do it when you start out, but word of mouth is some of the best advertising once it gets going."

Francie Greth-Peto says of marketing and promotion, "We had a free ride for a while. Because we were doing something new, we had a lot of free publicity. That's not the case any more. Llama packing is still interesting, and the press still likes to know about it, but it's not new. So you have to sell your business, you have to know how to make that work.

"One of the most effective things is to keep a real high profile in your community. Do a lot of outreach. Just get those llamas out there so people know you are around. Initially we did a lot of outreach. We took our llamas places, put a pack on them and took them to the fair.

"Our mailing list has been our most effective source. That grew by word of mouth, by past press releases and information in newspapers. There are good mailing lists that can be rented, but we only did that once. We advertise in newspapers and in the travel sections of national magazines, and that's been real helpful. You have to advertise, you have to let people know you're there."

Llama packers generally use a brochure, to be mailed out, often with full-color photos of friendly llamas, happy hikers, and glorious scenery. One attractive full-color brochure was put out by the Colorado Llama Outfitters and Guides Association. It contains an insert with descriptions of the several different llama trekking businesses that make up the association. I'm sure there were excellent economies of scale for the businesses in going in together, and the cooperation is nice to see. The Colorado Tourist Board has promoted llama packing in that state.

Pleasing the customers

Tom Landis said, "I think the important thing is the ability to manage people in the wilderness. There are a lot of people who have tried to start llama packing businesses and are not doing it any more. I think some of those people were undercapitalized. A lot of them didn't realize that they had to promote it. But the critical factor to me is having experience at managing people in the wilderness. You need to make sure the people are safe, comfortable, and happy.

"The llamas are a way to assist you with that. They make it easy for the people to get where you want to take them. They are a

Pleasing the customers includes many activities. Stanlynn Daugherty wades across a river with a string of llamas, while guests stroll across a footbridge.

gimmick which allows you to sell your trip as something different. And they bring people back. The people fall in love with the animals.

"I have a lot of repeat customers. It's partly the llamas. But I've talked to people who have gone on other llama trips and won't go back to those packers because they didn't enjoy the trip. The outfitter didn't do a good job. You have to treat the people well and give them the confidence that you know how to handle anything that's going to come up in the wilderness. We seldom have any problems. Part of not having any problems is preventing them from happening."

Many of the commercial packers had experiences that helped them with this end of things. Tom Landis had been a high school teacher with a sideline business of taking teenagers on backpacking trips in the high Sierra for a number of years.

Stanlynn Daugherty had been a travel agent. "You have to be very well organized," she says. "That's a key ingredient for sure. I can get the animals organized, I can get the meals prepared, I can get all the camp chores done. Also people need to be entertained on a certain level."

Francie Greth-Peto concurs. "You need to treat people so that they will want to come back. Even if they never do, they're going to spread the word about llama packing in general and about your business specifically. If they didn't have a good time, that's not going to be real good news. There are times that we can't be comfortable in the wilderness, but at least you have to facilitate the environment for people. You have to have people skills. I've learned a lot about living with people full-time."

There are numerous preparation details, Francie points out. "Getting ready for a pack trip, I can work for twelve to fifteen hours, buying the food, pre-preparing it, getting the equipment ready. The last thing I do is catch the llamas. That's easy! That's fun. All the rest of it takes so much more time and dedication, and it has nothing to do with llamas. It has to do with food services and creating a comfortable travelling environment for people."

Sometimes it rains.

Making money at llama packing

None of the packers that I talked to make their living solely off llama packing. One or two thought it was theoretically possible. Francie Greth-Peto commented, "I think most people would be hard pressed to make their entire living off llama packing. There are a finite number of days in the year that you can be out on the trail, there are a finite number of people that you can take on a trip, and there is a limit to what they will pay. If you look at our predecessors, horse and mule packers, you'll find that it's not a moneyed profession. But you can definitely generate some income."

A number of llama packers are also breeders. Every now and then, they say, they sell an animal to a trip customer, but overall that isn't much of a market.

Another llama packer had a different approach to thinking about the income. Since both he and his wife made good salaries, they weren't excited about making money to be taxed at high rates. What with buying animals, packs, food, a horse trailer, and so on, their llama packing business tends to run in the red. But that has given them tax deductions which have yielded them several thousand dollars in money that had been withheld from their salaries. They are quite content with this arrangement. A business does need to make a profit some years or else it's at risk of being declared a hobby by the IRS, but this worked for a while for them.

What is it going to cost to start a packing business? How soon can you see a profit? The sidebar shows a worksheet you can use to estimate income and expenses.

The income depends on how many trips are given, what is charged per trip, and the number of customers who go out. The number of trips will reflect the climate, what else is demanding your time in the season, how many people are working, and other factors. The charges range. Stanlynn Daugherty's Hurricane Creek Llama Treks offers trips of five, six, and seven days at $535, $640, and $750 respectively; those are 1993 prices. Hurricane Creek Llamas also offers shorter trips for teaching people to pack with llamas, in which participants provide their own food and camping gear.

Many packers took friends out at little or no cost for the first year or two. This gave them practical experience in being out with people and llamas.

WORKSHEET: LLAMA PACKING INCOME AND EXPENSES

ITEM	YR 1	YR 2	YR 3

INCOME
Pack trips
Sale of llamas
Misc.

  TOTAL INCOME:

EXPENSES
Purchase llamas
Feed, vet care
Boarding
Fencing, sheds
Equipment
Insurance:
  Llamas
  Liability
Vehicle, trailer
Legal, prof. advice
Govt permit fees
Marketing:
  Brochure
  Direct mail
  Ads
  Other
Food for trips
Employees
Office expenses

  TOTAL EXPENSE:

  PROFIT OR LOSS:

Sale of llamas isn't likely to be a major factor at first. Later, when certain llamas have acquired trail experience, you may want to sell them. Experienced pack llamas can command good prices.

Miscellaneous income could include the sale of llama wool, llama books and videotapes, tee-shirts, etc.

There's a long list of expenses. If you are buying llamas, expect to pay $500 to $2000 per packer, depending on quality and training. How many animals you'll need will vary with circumstances. You may want to add one or two each year, letting the younger ones learn from the older ones and selling off the ones that aren't exactly right for you.

Stanlynn Daugherty, who grows some of her own hay, told me once that her feed and vet bills ran about $75 a year per animal. We had to buy all our hay, and we spent about $125 per animal for feed alone; our vet bills weren't usually enormous. If you have to board animals out, there will be an ongoing charge there. If you have a farm where they can live, will you have to spend money to upgrade the facilities?

Equipment includes llama packs, sleeping bags, pads, and tents, llama halters, lead ropes, stake-out lines, buckets, cooking gear, and so forth.

Insurance costs can be large. More than one would-be packer's arithmetic has taken a nose-dive into the red right here. One woman who knew I was writing this book wrote to me, "I hope very much you will have some constructive advice on insurance. I don't mean on animals, but on liability! In our 'sue-happy' society, how can one still hope to make a profit after paying the exorbitant insurance premiums?"

Kelly and I couldn't. Insurance was one of the reasons we stopped doing our day hikes business. When we had insurance, it didn't matter that we were only doing hikes for four months of the year. The insurance companies would insure us for twelve months or not at all. We were told that llamas were lumped in with all outfitters and guides, including river rafters.

Shopping around is always advisable. Jay Rais commented, "When I looked into liability insurance so I could lease some of my trained llamas, I was told I would have to pay the same rate as a horse or mule packer. That's nuts. You don't ride llamas; they don't bite and rarely kick. So how can they be considered as dangerous as horses on the trail?"

It seems that rates have fallen somewhat. A packer who had to pay $1200 in 1990 told me that figure had dropped to $780 for 1993.

Anyone transporting llamas to a trailhead needs one or more vehicles. Pickups with stock racks and vans can carry llamas, or they can ride in a trailer. Equipment and guests will also need to be transported.

Legal and professional advice might be needed; for example, would you want to incorporate? Other matters could benefit from an accountant's comments.

Marketing is an area where you can spend a major fortune or do it on a shoestring. Peter Illyn traded llama hikes for many of his needs, including the creation of his logo, the printing of his advertising, and a musician's sound track for his slide show. He has also swapped llama packing for booth space at trade shows on outdoor activities. He has offered free trips as prizes for political fund-raising auctions, and commented that those gave his business lots of exposure.

If you hire employees, the costs go well beyond what you pay them. You will have state and federal regulations concerning what kind of insurance you carry on them, for both unemployment and your liability should they be injured on the job. While many of the more established packers do have employees, few people start out with them.

Office expenses are another figure. Do you already have a computer for keeping your books, your mailing list, form letters, etc.? I'm such a big fan of computers that I can't imagine running a business without one, though I realize people did it for centuries.

As you total these figures up and run them out for a few years, you should get some idea of the range of possibilities. One llama owner who didn't start a packing business estimated it would have taken him around ten thousand dollars in start-up capital. It can take a few years to get up to a level of business where you're in the black.

Some llama packers have expanded their business to include more exotic travel. When the Peruvian political situation was better, there were trips to South America, which include a city portion going to places of special interest to llama owners and a trekking portion going high in the Andes with Indian guides and llamas. More recently,

Stanlynn Daugherty takes a group annually on a seven-day llama trek in the French alps—staying in small mountain village hostels—with llama breeder and packer Christiane Giudicelli of Les Lamas du Buech in southeastern France.

Llama day hikes

In the mid-1980s, Kelly and I took people for day hikes with llamas, on our ranch. It required a conditional use permit from the county, which took several months and the help of a consultant to obtain. We took out a bank loan to start the hikes and to buy more llamas. We built trails, experimented with recipes, trained the llamas, did a brochure, got lots of good local publicity, and welcomed the public.

It was much less work than going out into the wilderness, which we didn't have the background or inclination for. We were home, could work on other projects as well, and just break for the hikes. We were quite busy in July and August, with June and September slower.

And it was fun. The pleasure that people took in the llamas was great. We did sometimes get tired of answering the same questions over and over, but it was easy to recognize that they were new questions to the person asking.

We charged between $20 and $35 per adult, half for children, and we offered a discount for groups of six or more. The price range reflected the duration of the trips, with the shortest being supposedly a couple of hours. They often went longer. We did them for as few as two people. We met a lot of very interesting people that way, and often were in no hurry to end the conversation over the picnic.

There were some advantages in our situation. We were fifteen minutes away from Ashland, Oregon, a tourist destination, and about half our business was from tourists. Also, our seventy-acre ranch was in a spectacularly beautiful setting, up in the mountains with views in every direction, Mount Shasta sparkling some fifty miles away. The air was fresh, and there was usually a pleasant little breeze. We offered two hikes, one quite level, and the other quite steep, each with a lovely picnic spot.

Being in the mountains did limit our season, though. It could snow as late as mid-June. A few hikes ended up with the meal being in our living room, when the weather changed quickly. Kelly had put a rock floor in the front of the living room, so the llamas came in with

us. Poco would happily hunker down on the rock floor, next to a cardboard box with some hay in it.

The second season, our hikes and a photo were in the ``Northwest Travel Guide" pages of the Northwest edition of *Sunset Magazine*. That one mention accounted for about half our business that year and some the next year.

We stopped the hikes after three years. We hadn't made much money. By then, our publishing company was expanding into videotapes, we were still building our house, and there was the herd to care for. We had to chose what would really get done.

We sold one llama to a hikes customer. Dancing Cloud, the first baby born to us, went to Edie Mattson, who lives not far away. When we later sold our ranch, it was purchased by a couple who had been on one of the hikes. They sent us some photos from the day they came hiking, and there was Edie in the photos! They had been on the same hike she had taken. Unbeknownst to us, a lot of seeds were planted that day.

Since then, I've kept an ear out for other people doing llama day hikes, as I do believe they can work in the right circumstances. Several commercial packers offer them as well as longer ones. Customers who take the day hikes may go on to greater adventures.

Jane Robertson-Boudreaux and Jerry Boudreaux did llama day hikes for two years into the Rocky Mountain National Park. It was an experimental program, and a great success in terms of the effect the llamas had on the Park Service and the future of llamas within it. Jane and Jerry did a lot of public education about llamas, both to their paying guests and to other tourists at the park. How was it financially? "We barely broke even," Jane told me.

The Future of llama packing

All the llama packers that I spoke with felt that there is room for more packers, in different parts of the country and offering a variety of kinds of trips. "Look at how many horse packers there are," Stanlynn Daugherty pointed out to me. There are a lot of people out there who would enjoy a llama pack trip." The numbers are likely to increase, as llamas become better known and as their light impact on the environment becomes more appreciated.

CHAPTER NINE:

What Else Can You Do With Llamas?

IT'S A SIGN of the growth of the llama industry that people are earning money doing a variety of activities related to llamas. In many cases, the individuals involved already owned llamas, and they formed an additional business, as we did in publishing llama books and videotapes and in starting a day hikes business. In other instances, the people found a way to be involved with the animals without actually owning them.

This chapter will describe activities suitable for earning just a few extra dollars to ones that are vast undertakings. As with any business, there can be a start-up period before you see a profit, but with the increasing popularity of llamas, many businesses are doing very well indeed. The opportunities for additional products and services are limited only by the imagination. Llama lovers are already showing a lot of that!

Wool

Wool is one source of income from llamas, but it is not a major one at this time. By the time you comb or shear a llama, remove debris from the wool which is usable and throw out quite a lot which isn't, you have something which can be sold at retail for around two dollars an ounce—quite high as wool prices go, but not necessarily enough to pay for the effort involved in collecting and cleaning it. I have heard llama owners say that they made enough to pay for their animals' feed through wool sales. As our llamas' feed costs have run around $10 per month per llama, that gives you an idea of the scale.

In the future, the market for llama wool is likely to increase considerably. Linda Berry Walker is a llama breeder coming from a strong background in the sheep and textile worlds. She has repeatedly pointed out, in articles and at conferences, that the demand for specialty fibers is booming all over the world. It is projected to continue booming well into the next century.

In some regions, llama owners have begun banding together to sell their wool to handspinners. In addition, various llama owners have talked with commercial woolen mills but so far nothing major has occurred. Because of the differences between llama wool and sheep's wool, the llama wool can't simply be run through the same processes.

So for now, it's a cottage industry. Many llama owners may be collecting the wool anyway, as they like to keep their animals looking

Lil Bit, our woolliest, is in front, before shearing.

After shearing, she looks quite slender.

nice, or they shear them to reduce heat stress. Sometimes handspinners will collect and perhaps clean the wool for a llama owner, in exchange for some of the wool.

People collect the wool using various tools. We've used a dog's wire slicker brush, usually after blowing the llama with a leaf blower. The slicker brush can pull, and should be used with attention to how it feels to the llama.

If the wool is full of twigs, bits of hay, or other debris, it's best to just throw it out right away. The process of cleaning llama wool is slow and tedious enough that perfectionists can go nuts. Shorter wool, from the lower legs and other places on the body, is not ordinarily used; how short is usable depends on the spinner's preference. Some neck wool is usable, on the longer-wooled animals. To be usable, llama wool really has to be very clean.

We sold llama wool that I had combed out, both to people who came to our ranch for hikes and through a local fiber arts store. I would clean it to some extent; we made around two hundred dollars a year from sales of wool. When I began learning to spin, I realized that the wool I'd prepared would indeed need more cleaning to be ready to spin.

Our ranch in the mountains never had much green pasture; llamas on nice pasture stay cleaner than ours did. Combining the llamas' love of rolling in the dust with their penchant for spilling bits of hay out of their feeders, and you can imagine the condition of our llamas' wool.

To clean the wool, I sit with a sheet over a table, and hand-pick the wool, that is, pull it apart, bit by bit, so that the debris falls out onto the table below. I like doing this in the daytime, with strong light coming in the window. After an hour or more of cleaning wool, I have a little pile of clean wool, my eyes and nose are a bit runny from breathing the dust, and I'm ready to do something else. But the spinning is such fun that I'm soon back to clean more wool. Recently I had my wool carded at a mill, so now I have lovely bags of ready-to-spin wool.

Many people have made beautiful things from the wool. Many items—hand-knit and hand-woven, felted, sometimes dyed—are displayed at llama conferences. Prices for such lovely things are generally quite high, but again not in proportion to the number of hours in the products. Llama wool is frequently mixed with wool from sheep, partly because the llama wool has much less elasticity than that of sheep.

Toni Landis cautions people that working with wool is time-consuming and not easily lucrative. "It's possible to make clothing yourself, but you have to get very high prices. I was a commercial handweaver and handspinner. I designed yarn, sweaters, and fabric. I also made clothing from the fabric and sold that. I would combine my llama wool with half sheep's wool because I like the feel of it better, it extends it. It's really nice. But I priced out my garments per ounce. And there was no way that I could collect wool from my llamas, put it in a garment, and sell the garment for anything under four or five hundred dollars. That's a very discretionary market."

Animal care and services

"I'd rather be in the rain and mud than in an office," llama trainer Reta Hamel said to me. She spoke for many people. Activities which provide contact with the animals include training, grooming, boarding, running a nursery, and transporting llamas. You can also work as a ranch hand, llama sitter, or ranch manager. Wherever there are llamas, there are need for these support services. In most areas of the country, there aren't a lot of people doing them.

"Right here in central Oregon, there's a big need for some training and grooming people," Averill Abbott told me as we talked at a LANA conference in Redmond. "People who want to go to shows may not have the time to groom their animals.

"Also there's a need to train some of these animals. You can take an inexpensive gelded male, teach him to pull a cart, get him to be a real nice animal to have around. It may take a little while to get it going, but I think that kind of business would be a good one. What kind of investment would you have to have? Just time and a few hundred dollars."

Helen Bodington is a llama trainer in San Anselmo, California, who will pick up llamas within about two hundred miles of her home. She brings them to her place for about three weeks, trains them there, and returns them to the owner. When she returns the animal, she spends an hour or two showing the owner what the llama has learned and encouraging the owner to continue training. When I talked with her, she charged $235 for an animal sixteen months and under and

$285 for one older than that; the prices include a copy of the training manual she wrote.

"If you wanted to train them to make your living," she said, "Probably one of the most important things would be to be where they are. There must be people all over the country who are attempting to do this."

I asked her about the qualities of a good trainer. She said patience and the ability to understand the llama from its body language and voice.

Some people buy male llamas, train them to pack or just to be easily handled, and then resell them. This provides a real service to llama owners who don't have the time or inclination to do these things themselves.

Boarding llamas is usually done for much less money per animal than boarding horses; see the discussion in Chapter Two. One llama owner who was considering starting up a boarding business estimated that he would be breaking even at fifty dollars per month per llama.

Sheron Herriges-Smith is a llama breeder who started a llama nursery in 1976. Hundreds of sick or orphaned babies have gotten a good start thanks to her care. With as many as twenty or thirty babies in residence, it has often been an around-the-clock activity keeping Sheron, her husband Bruce, and a full-time helper busy.

I asked if somebody could make a living at it.

She wasn't encouraging. "Bruce and I figure that we make about $2.50 an hour—and that's on a good day! That's probably why nobody else is doing it."

Phone calls further break up the days; while I was talking with Sheron, three other calls came in. If anyone with the skills, energy, and resources wanted to take on such a challenge, Sheron would encourage them to do it. The need is certainly there, and is going to grow with the llama population. I would add that they'd better have nurturing instincts that just don't quit!

Transporting llamas is another service that is growing with the increase in the national llama market. Llama owners may buy a llama at a distant auction or ranch, and have it transported rather than doing the hauling themselves. Some of the people offering this service are llama owners themselves, so they understand the animals.

For someone who lives in an area where there are llamas, working on a ranch is an excellent way to get to know the animals. Many ranches can use help, and while the tasks may start with shovelling out the barn, they are likely to progress to other things as well.

Sometimes people help out on ranches for no pay, just to learn. I'm sure lots of ranches would be interested in this arrangement! I've known people to swap their labor, skilled or unskilled, for stud service or partial payment on llamas.

Llama sitters are often friends, neighbors, relatives, or employees of llama owners who get pressed into service. One woman I know charges $10 a day for house-sitting with domestic pets and $20 a day for small ranches. The price includes her sleeping over. A single person or a couple who had the temperament and flexibility for it might make a living llama-sitting all over the country, once they acquired the necessary skills and reputation. There would be some drawbacks: you would never get to go to a llama conference, as that's when sitters are in greatest demand, and there might be more winter calls from cold places than from balmy ones. Someone who did this for a while might be hired someplace permanently.

Some of the larger ranches hire ranch managers who oversee the entire llama operation. The duties and pay vary.

Using llamas

There are surveyors who use llamas to carry thousands of dollars of expensive surveying equipment. Since llamas are so surefooted and dependable—especially if chosen with attention to their individual natures—they can be used in situations where other pack animals wouldn't even be considered. The alternatives would be the surveyor's own back or, in one situation I heard about, helicopters.

This use draws on the traditional uses of llamas through the centuries. They've been pack animals for thousands of years. Another packing use, besides running an actual pack business, would be to lease llamas, to the Forest Service or to individuals. One problem with this is that the insurance costs may be the same as for running a pack business, so it's not something that can easily be undertaken on a tiny scale.

Two other traditional llama products in South America are their dung and their meat. Very few North Americans are prepared to eat llama. I do know of one llama who ended up in the freezer after lightning struck a tree which fell on the animal. I like the idea of using an animal fully, harking back to Native American respect for the totality of the animal. If a berserk male had to be killed, I could see using the meat. I can respect that llamas are an important source of meat in South America, but using llamas for meat is likely to remain rare here. It's an emotionally charged issue. Many people were drawn to owning llamas—rather than other livestock—precisely because llamas are not normally destined to be eaten.

Llama manure is quite useful. In the high plains of the Andes, few trees grow, and the dung is burned as a source of fuel. Here, the manure is applied to gardens as a fertilizer. At one time or another, llama owners in Oregon, California, and New York—and probably other places—have put it through a screen, dried, and bagged it or dissolved it in water and sold it as LlaManure, Llama Poo, or some other cute name.

Some of the other uses that llamas are being put to are not likely to have been done in the Andes. Florence Dix of the Seattle area is one llama owner who has been written up in *Llamas* for her activities. She takes her geldings to all kinds of social events, from birthday parties to conventions. She has a flair for PR—and a lot of fun. At around $50 (plus travel costs) an outing, this sounds like a great merger of llamas for love and for money. At least one therapist includes his llamas in his work. Several bed-and-breakfasts have llamas as part of their attraction.

Guard llamas

Yet another use of the llama holds great promise for the sheep industry. Erma Hast tells in *Llama Life* of three different sheep ranchers who each ran one gelded llama with their herds of a thousand or more sheep—and cut their large losses from coyotes down to nothing or close to it. One rancher reported that his llama wouldn't allow strange people or dogs—let alone coyotes—among the herd. Erma told me that young males placed with sheep have worked out beautifully, and she thinks this could be a good outlet for male llamas, and a chance for them to do really useful work. Adult male llamas are also being introduced to sheep-herding; time will tell if they adapt as well as the youngsters.

Research is ongoing on these topics. In one study of sheep ranchers—see Chapter 12, Resource Guide, for the Iowa State University pamphlet reporting on this—they had been losing an average of 26 sheep per year, mostly to coyotes and dogs. After adding guard llamas to their flocks, losses dropped to an average of 8 sheep per year. Half the 145 ranchers saw their losses drop to zero.

Some llamas would not be suited to the task. Male llamas who were experienced breeders might try to breed the female sheep; after all, our male llama Poco tried to breed our female Komondor guard dog. Also, as llama owners generally are so careful to keep from exposing our llamas to dogs, there does need to be an awareness of the risk to the llamas in guarding the sheep, to consider with the evident benefit that they can provide to the sheep.

Marketing llamas

Some people buy llamas to resell, while others put buyers and sellers in touch with each other for a fee. Others act as marketing consultants or advisers. These are not activities for a beginner; you need to know llamas well and have a good reputation.

Photography and art

Whether for advertising or simply for pleasure, llamas are being photographed constantly. The best-known llama photographer, Susan Jones Ley, says, "There's a market for aspiring llama photographers. People's ads are getting very sophisticated, and a simple snapshot just doesn't make it any more.

"I'd say to someone wanting to do this that the first rule of good llama photography is an understanding of the subject. Visit llama farms in your area, and look at lots of llamas through the viewfinder without taking any pictures at all. Learn how llamas walk, how they react, what kinds of things they do at different times of the day. Now that there are llama farms all over the country, you don't have to travel great distances to learn the craft.

"This is a very difficult field to make money in. I do, but I've been at it for thirteen years. When a breeder spends a lot of time grooming animals for a shoot, he wants results, not excuses. So you have to be good at this before you start to develop a clientele.

"In addition to being good at taking photographs of llamas, you have to have energy and lots of it. I can't tell you the number of shoots I've done where I end up working eighteen hour days.

"Then there's the weather. If it's bad, you have to solve extremely difficult technical problems and you have to do it in a hurry. The owners are expecting results no matter what, and they've already paid a great deal to fly you to their location. So you have to be able to do the job and you have to have the confidence that you can. That boils down to being able to handle heavy duty stress and lots of it!

"The best way to develop a clientele is to give away free pictures. I found it helpful to be very generous in giving away photographs. It's the best way to get your name out there in front of the public, to have your pictures circulating. You can put a copyright stamp on the back of them so they can't legally be reproduced.

"You've got to work with a medium format camera to do this job. A lot of owners will want large posters of their animals, and 35mm just won't get the sharpness you need. Throw the two formats

Lally investigates photographer Steve Johnson.

together, and it's a real mental job to keep adjusting back and forth between them."

Susan told me that there is a need for photography for notecards, postcards, calendars, stock houses, and magazines. She has done this kind of thing—the first llama poster featured one of her photographs—and she has also published a book of photography featuring llama farms across the country. (It's listed in the Resource Guide.)

There are also photographic possibilities for people with less skill. There is supposedly a man who takes his llama and a Polaroid camera into downtown Manhattan, and makes quite a sum by taking instant pictures of people with the llama. I've heard this story for years. So has Marty McGee, formerly of upstate New York, who comments, "I've never talked to the person, so I don't know, but I've heard it from too many people for it to be a myth. Of course, that's how myths happen!"

Myth or reality, the idea can be applied.

Many artists have used llamas for models. Katie Emrich of Sisters, Oregon, began drawing llamas.

"The first llamas that I drew were so incredibly ugly. They looked like goats. Danny used to stand over my shoulder, use my eraser, and erase part off my picture right off the page. Then he'd explain to me what actually happened under the wool, about the joints and bones and whatnot."

Once she got the llama pictures to her satisfaction, it was a natural next step to market various products. Among her best-known are tee-shirts marketed by the Shirt Stop in Sisters, and sold at many conferences. "It has been absolutely imperative each year to have new, fresh stuff. And of course, all the old screens are still available. But all the return customers will come to see what's new. If we had the same thing over and over again, we'd be in a down spiral for sure." She commented later, "I've got some talented competition out there. But that's good!"

Katie has done custom paintings of llamas for people, but doesn't any more. There are other people who do this, and there will be more. We had a booth at a LANA conference next to artist Jane Marek, and I was fascinated to watch her work from color photos of llamas. She has also done a number of wonderful llama cartoons, which reflect her knowledge of the animals.

Considering how beautiful llamas are to start with, how enamored of them their owners often are, and the amount of disposable income within the llama community, the income possibilities for good llama photography and art are great.

Publications

Francie Greth-Peto and her husband Guy Peto began a little newsletter called *The 3-L Llama* (after an Ogden Nash poem) in 1979. By the third issue that year, they had forty subscribers. That issue consisted of seven typewritten pages enlivened with drawings and one photocopied photograph.

"There were so few people who had llamas," Francie said. "So we couldn't find any information. What we could find didn't seem relevant, a few facts in an encyclopedia that didn't make a whole lot of difference to our life. So we were anxious to find out what other people were doing. Each llama owner we met, we asked them if they knew any others, and that way we found ten people. Our first letter was produced on my school's little purple spirit ditto master, and went out to those ten people. Within three years, the subscribership grew to close to four hundred. As the interest in the newsletter was really growing, there was a time factor; we had to choose between the newsletter and packing. We sold the newsletter to Bob and Cheryl Dal Porto. They maintained the name for a while, and then made a wise decision to change the name."

And thus was *Llamas* born. Current issues contain over a hundred pages, many with color photographs, and include numerous articles, departments, ads, and so on. Now there are other periodicals as well; the most notable is *Llama Life*, a black and white quarterly in newspaper format, published by Terry and Kathy Price, which has carved out a unique position for itself. *Llama Banner* is a colorful glossy emphasizing shows.

Francie feels there's room for several periodicals. "Look at the equine world. Look at how many horse magazines there are. If people have a real interest in something, they usually subscribe to more than one magazine. I get at least two computer magazines a month!"

I would extend her comment to books and videotapes as well. Several years ago, I did a list for the International Llama Association of everything in print for a general audience on lamas—that is, llamas, alpacas, vicunas, and guanacos. There wasn't much. Recently I updated the list. The flowering of lama publishing was evident! Many of the books and videotapes are self-published. They vary in publishing sophistication, and there are things in some of them that I totally disagree with, but every one of them contributes something to our knowledge of llamas.

I think our experience with Juniper Ridge Press has been typical of many of the small businesses, publishing and otherwise, that have grown up around llamas.

I unload 3,000 copies of my first book.

We didn't set out to start a llama publishing company. *Living with Llamas*, my first book, grew out of the journal I kept for the first couple of years that we had llamas. I used to be a librarian, and I thought it would be fun to write and publish a book about llamas. The book came out just before Christmas 1984, and I mailed a flyer to the several hundred people then on my mailing list. Within a short time I had made back my printing bill of several thousand dollars, and the book was selling steadily. This was helped along by a favorable review in *Booklist*, a magazine for librarians, which led to orders for the book from libraries all across the nation. Best of all, many people enjoyed my book—and bought llamas after reading it!

The next year, my husband Kelly acquired video equipment to go to the Soviet Union and make some programs. After he had done that, he went out to the pasture and started making llama videotapes.

In the book world generally, only about half the books published show a profit; we have not felt we could afford to publish a book or tape that wouldn't be profitable, so we've chosen our topics to meet what we thought were the major needs. I was particularly happy to bring out Stanlynn Daugherty's book, *Packing with Llamas*.

We still do almost everything ourselves, from our home. One nice thing about creating books and videotapes is that they continue to make money for you while you're working on another project. We have made far more money from our publications than from our llamas.

There are many needed llama books and videotapes. I'll toss out two ideas we had, for anyone else to pick up. We played around with the idea of a llama video magazine, to come out perhaps quarterly, and to have informative sections that people would want to refer back to, such as how to trim toenails, or showing a birth, as well as current news, such as the top llamas at an auction. The ads could be visually very interesting too, showing llamas at various ranches. Such a video magazine could be done with high-end consumer equipment; it wouldn't be profitable if the production costs were high.

I wish somebody would come out with a thorough, detailed index to the llama periodicals, a sort of *Reader's Guide to Periodicals* for llamas and alpacas. As I looked through my many back issues of all the periodicals in the course of researching one thing or another for this book, I was impressed with how much valuable information is in them. It would be a real service to create easier access to it.

The publications all serve the purpose of sharing information. Another way to share information is to put on workshops. This is done on a national scale by the llama organizations, on a regional scale by local groups and individuals, and on a local scale by individuals. Just about all of these can be profitable as well as a real service. I've taught "Llamas for Love and Money" through Continuing Education at a local college, and many other people have done similar things.

Llama equipment and gift items

Adjustable llama halters, packs designed to fit the contours of a llama's back, carts for driving, special forms for ranch record-keeping, computer software for the same purpose, baby blankets for little crias—many creative hours have gone into designing and marketing these and other products designed especially for llamas. The array of llama packs is astonishing for such a small industry! Then there are all the items that are used with llamas that were already manufactured, such as the blowers people use to remove debris from their llamas' wool.

And the gift items! Beautiful or schlocky, decorative or useful, there are many, many items available. Weathervanes, tee-shirts, jewelry, ranch banners, pottery, toilet seat covers, customized license plate holders, potholders, Andean imports, upscale stuffed toy llamas—a profusion of items are available, more every year. Sometimes I think that llamas might catch on as a symbol, the way unicorns did. Will we someday encounter sketched llamas as ubiquitous as the smiley face? I hope it doesn't go quite that far.

Marketing llama-related items

It's relatively easy to find your target audience if you market something to do with llamas. Ads in the magazines, having a booth at ILA and other conferences, and perhaps some direct mail will do it. Once you get started, word of mouth will help any popular item.

There are several businesses that market a variety of items to the llama community. Quality Llama Products (formerly Llamas and More) was a pioneer in this field. Rocky Mountain Llamas carries equipment, much of it designed by Bobra Goldsmith, and some publications. LLasa LLamas carries tack, publications, and miscellany. *Llamas* has a store, a listing of publications and gift items that they sell by mail and at their store in California. The list is printed in the magazine, with an order form. (The Resource Guide in the back of this book gives addresses for these places. There are a number of others, generally smaller, that you can discover in the pages of the llama magazines and at the conferences.)

One thing that I've really enjoyed about doing business within the llama community has been the enthusiastic and responsive people. In our first few years of selling products by mail, we had something like three bad checks. The first one was a bank error, and the others got taken care of quickly.

It will be fun to see how all these auxiliary llama businesses come along in the future. If you have a good product or service, you can start small and grow.

CHAPTER TEN

Llamas as an Investment

HOW MUCH MONEY can people make with llamas?

It depends.

One woman wrote to me, "For several years, I've been interested in raising llamas. We have raised horses, and had a large pig farm twenty-five years ago. I raise German Angora rabbits for the wool, and I grow everlastings which I plan to go into on a larger scale. We operate a bed and breakfast on our ranch. I am a vegetarian, so I'm extremely interested in raising animals for purposes other than butchering."

For someone like this, who already has the land, the skills, and the desire, llamas can become profitable members of the family

For people who think it would be nice to move to the country and to have some llamas, a lot more pieces of the puzzle will have to fall into place before they'll see a profit.

How much money you might make with llamas depends on several things.

It depends on what types of llamas you buy, and which specific animals you select. It depends on how fertile and healthy they and their offspring are. It depends on the quality of care you provide for them. It depends on your overhead costs. It depends on your marketing, and on the choices you make about which animals you will sell.

In large measure, it depends on what you do. As Averill Abbott puts it, "Time, money, acreage, and commitment are all factors to consider." So investing in llamas, like starting any other business, is investing in your own abilities and choices.

It also depends on a variety of factors over which you have no control: the overall economy, if llamas are imported from South America in any significant numbers, the weather, etc.

The weather is a real wild card these days. I suspect it's related to global warming, but whether it is or not, it's certainly been more erratic. This adds uncertainty to any agricultural activity. Llamas are very easy keepers in terms of their water needs, and they tolerate cold well and heat relatively poorly. How do you consider the weather in your decision-making, or do you? This will be a more serious question in some regions than in others.

If ten families all carefully researched llamas and decided they wanted to raise them, and if they all purchased llamas at around the same time, and if each family purchased, say, ten females and some studs, and if they all still owned llamas after ten years, how would their experiences compare at the end of that time?

Surely some would have done much better than others. This variation would reflect the skills and attitudes of the people as well as the luck of the draw.

If you looked at another ten families who had all purchased, say, three female llamas each, I would expect an even greater range of returns, because with smaller herds, the luck of the draw becomes a more significant factor and marketing is more difficult.

When I was writing the first edition of this book in 1989 and 1990, llama prices were going up and up, and many breeders were making large returns on their investments. Many people feared that prices might drop—"will the bubble burst?"—while others felt things were out of hand, and hoped they would drop.

It happened. Many prices are now half, or less than half, of what they were in 1990. I've been told that the market has fallen by the highest percentage for the high-end llamas.

"In the 1980s, there was a skewed inflation of values," one llama breeder said to me recently. "A lot of big-time operators paid big prices and expected to sell at even higher prices. Ordinary folks were happy enough to make lots of money. Then suddenly the economy—which had had nothing to do with llamas in the 1980s—came into our awareness. A lot of investors jumped ship—some of them made money, some of them lost, some broke even, but they all ended up with a dim outlook on the llama industry. Now, it's more real. I think all of us can make money if we see what has happened and adjust our prices. All kinds of people are buying llamas: backpackers, active seniors, many others."

The recession was probably the main factor that brought llama prices down. While I think they may slowly rise again—llamas are as wonderful and lovable as they ever were—one obvious benefit is that many people can now afford llamas who couldn't before. People who could only afford a few llamas can now have more. Lynn Hyder commented, "I started out when you could buy a nice female llama for fifteen hundred dollars. As the price went up, I saw potential customers fall by the wayside." Now, the number of potential customers is larger again.

The drawback is that it is now much more difficult to make a living from llamas alone. Some people are doing it, but many who used to or were trying to are now planning on llamas providing part of their incomes.

Later in this chapter, we'll use spreadsheets to look further at the question of how much money you might make with llamas.

Although I speak of llamas in this chapter, much of it can be applied also to alpacas. They appear to be more profitable at this

Alpacas are often a good investment. Cute, too!

point, with more income and less work per animal than llamas (but also higher investment costs); see Chapter 7 for further discussion of the business aspects of alpacas.

Llama prices

What are llama prices like? At this writing, as I said in Chapter five, you can find nice young males for pets or packing beginning around $500, sometimes less. Stud-quality males would begin around $1500, more for woolly ones. Sound females can be found as low as $2,500. These figures are the very lowest I've heard; if you paid $1000 for a young male to be trained as a packer, $5000 for a future stud, and $4000 for a nice weanling female, those would also be moderate prices.

Prices could be different by the time you read this. To get a sense of the range of prices, read the ads in the llama magazines—*Llama Link* is a free magazine, primarily consisting of ads—and read the articles as well. *Llama Life* editor Terry Price has very interesting analyses of auction prices in particular.

One factor working toward lower llama prices is the increasing number of animals. If there are somewhere above fifty thousand llamas in the United States, as Registrar Jack Thomas of the International Lama Registry estimated in 1992, put that figure in context. According to the US Census, there were over two million farms in the US in 1987; if you just count farms of less than fifty acres, there were almost six hundred thousand. These figures only count actual working farms; they don't include the numerous rural residences with acreage. Many of the farms and the residences could easily accommodate a herd of llamas, and many of their owners would love to have llamas.

Lynn Hyder observed, "Look at the size of this country. I flew to Minnesota and down to Wisconsin, and I looked at that land with all those little farms and those rural areas. There are thousands of cities in this country, and around them are suburbs where people have three, or ten, or fifteen acres. Everywhere, people like animals. There's a market out there that hasn't even been touched!"

Uncertainty regarding importation

Llamas were imported into the United States from time to time until the late 1920s, when our government made it illegal for ruminants to be imported from countries where foot and mouth disease, or FMD as it is usually abbreviated, is endemic. FMD is a viral disease highly contagious to livestock. In the following decades, occasionally some animals were imported from Europe, but essentially the US population developed with little outside breeding.

In 1983, the United States Department of Agriculture accepted Chile's assertion that it was free of FMD, and since then llamas and alpacas have been imported intermittently, through a high-security quarantine center. But in 1984 and again in 1987 outbreaks of FMD were reported by Chile. Both cases were reputed to be due to smuggling of animals across Chile's many miles of unguarded borders with neighboring countries which have endemic FMD.

In 1989 a branch of the USDA, the Animal and Plant Health Inspection Service (APHIS), again moved to declare Chile free of FMD, proposing that lamas (particularly llamas and alpacas) could be imported through any US quarantine station. The controls would be much looser than they have been to date. There is evidence that these controls might not be sufficient to keep FMD out of the United States.

Llama breeders have been following these events closely. In 1989, ILA protested to APHIS more vigorously than ever before, with over a thousand letters from concerned llama owners sent to APHIS. ILA has been working on this issue in a variety of ways, with members digging deeply into their pockets to finance the efforts. It has retained legal counsel. Many llama owners have written to their congressmen, and there has been concern voiced by some of these lawmakers. Other livestock and veterinary organizations have been contacted and become involved as well.

What are the implications of importation for llama and alpaca breeders in this country? When the first importation occurred, many breeders were concerned about health issues, and they worried that it would hurt the economics of llama breeding. There have as yet been no serious public health problems, and the business of breeding has continued. Breeders flocked to buy the imports, which generally went for high prices. The alpaca industry here got its start from imports of recent years.

After half a century with a small gene pool in North America, many breeders have been happy to have totally unrelated animals to breed to their domestic ones. Since nothing was known of the parentage of the South American animals, their use has not been without genetic risks.

There has been some perception by the press and the general public that lama (llama and alpaca) breeders are looking out for their own economic self-interest in calling for protectionism. Naturally, if the North American market were flooded with lower-priced imports, it could make a difference to breeders here. But also, FMD is a nasty disease. In countries where it is endemic, it is not always fatal but even when it doesn't cause death, its victims are weakened and vulnerable to other diseases. The virus can travel through the air for miles. If lamas were the inadvertent cause of FMD entering the US, there would be enormous suffering—and how do you think other livestock industries would feel toward us? The health and the economic aspects are intertwined. FMD isn't the only possible disease, either.

Two good ways to stay current on this situation are to join ILA, which sends its members reports and calls for action, and to read the llama periodicals.

Llamas and the economy

Several years ago, llama breeder Bob Niccolls was laid up for a few months with a back injury. He spent a lot of time reading and researching economic issues, a lifelong interest of his, ever since he got his degree in economics at Stanford. "The more I read, the more I think that we are setting ourselves up in this country for some desperate economic times. I'm anticipating a major recession or depression."

"So how do you tie this in to llamas? I believe that everyone to the extent possible should have a very conservative approach to their own financial well-being. A firm financial base is the best investment one can make. If people are borrowing on the house, or against the kids' education, to buy llamas, that is speculative."

Bob told me that when he and his wife Marty decided to become serious llama breeders, he burned his calculator to a frazzle, figuring out the cost factors.

His conclusions? Even with some decrease in llama prices, "I figured it sure as heck was a lot better than alfalfa. It wasn't a whole lot worse than my success with the stock market, and it was fun. We decided to do it, because we so enjoyed the animals."

Bob's conclusion reminded me of some charts I'd seen, done by John Schreiber. He analyzed llamas as an investment at varying price levels, including two rather drastic price drops. Both of those still do show a positive return on investment, albeit a small one, and the scenarios he develops of steady or rising prices show a strong return.

Llamas compared with other investments

Often when people ask how good an investment llamas are, they are comparing llamas in their minds with other money-making investments such as other unusual animals, real estate, stocks, and just plain savings. But sometimes they are choosing between llamas and consumer items, be it pickup trucks or expensive vacations. Compared to just about any consumer item, llamas are a top-notch investment!

Bob and Marty Niccolls invested in llamas.

Keep in mind that there are several aspects to analyze in choosing an investment: think about tax advantages or disadvantages, the safety of your initial investment, liquidity, current income, and long-term yield.

How do llamas compare with other animals? Llamas are sometimes compared with Arabian horses, often in a gloomy way by people who comment that the llama prices will drop as drastically as the prices for Arabians did. But llama owners who have bred—or are still breeding—Arabians, observe that there are far, far more Arabians than llamas and that the promotion of Arabians has reached levels not known in the llama world.

Exotics in general are popular. If you are drawn to emus or miniature donkeys or whatever, they could be worth investigating. Considering my history of coming home with animals I've gone to look at, I didn't dare do much research!

Kelly and I did visit a miniature donkey farm in our area, and it seemed to us that they would be delightful animals to own and get to know. They might well be a good choice for someone uncomfortable with the size of llamas. I don't know how the finances stack up.

Real estate is another investment to compare with llamas. Jack Meyers told me, "I was in just about every phase of real estate. With llamas, you don't have to have the sophistication and the education that you need in the complex real estate investments. Real estate was a good investment for us, because we were in it at the right time.

"Of course, investing in real estate does depend a great deal on the location, whereas investing in the llama business doesn't. You can raise llamas anywhere, which is a nice feature.

"Real estate is a good type of investment for certain people, because it's tangible. People are also interested in precious metals, because that's something they can touch and see. The animals, of course, react to you, whereas those things don't. That's what we've enjoyed so much. When you express your appreciation and your love for them, they return it."

His wife Dee commented, "There's not any investment other than animals that you can do that with, is there?"

Jack said, "It might be a couple of centuries before llamas would be as numerous as horses are now. We've heard that there are over twelve million registered horses in the United States, not counting the backyard horses. Llamas are a long way from that."

What about stocks and bonds? I was once chatting with a stockbroker after a talk she had given on socially responsible investments. I said that I had an investment free of military or polluting implications: a herd of llamas. "Now there's a high-risk investment!" was her immediate response.

Dr. Ralph Uber, who has bred both llamas and alpacas, told me, "I personally feel that alpacas are a better investment than anything I know of, but I think people are sometimes anxious to get a return immediately. They should realize that it probably takes about three years to start getting a return. Of course, if you're going to build up your herd, you're not going to get a return for some time."

Several years ago, stockbroker George Peoples had called me from his home in Virginia, to ask my opinion of the behavior of a llama, who turned out to be a berserk male. Having weathered that experience, he and his wife Debbie now have a herd of llamas. Later I turned the tables on him, asking for his comments on llamas, stocks, and investing in general.

"The money you put into llamas should actually be discretionary," he began. "I encourage new breeders to take full mortality insurance, which is around four percent of the value of an animal—they can think of it like sales tax the first year—and to buy animals that the breeder will guarantee as to reproductive capacity." When those steps are taken, George didn't consider llamas to be a high-risk investment.

"If you buy llamas with all the money you've got, you could get into trouble. There are overhead costs. I tell people not to expect to take any money out for five years."

George pointed out that there will always be people with discretionary income for llamas, and there will always be some people in financial trouble.

George mused, "Why do investors buy an original painting for a fortune when they could buy a print for a fraction of the cost? There is something special about the painting. Llamas are kind of like that. After all, goats are lovable too. But when I go down to my barn and just sit with my llamas, the emotional and even spiritual relationship I feel with them is unique."

George ended our phone call with one last word: "Diversify!"

I suggest you also compare llamas with the plain old unglamorous savings fund, often held in money market accounts or

CDs at a local bank. There's a nifty principle for figuring approximately how long it will take to double your invested funds: the ``rule of 72'' states that if you divide the interest rate into 72, the number you get is close to the number of years it will take, assuming that you leave the earned interest in to compound. So if you are getting 6%, your funds should double in about twelve years. Those ten hypothetical families could have left their money in savings and if they were getting 6% interest, in twelve years, they would have doubled their money. Not counting taxes. And there are considerable tax advantages to a llama business.

How would llamas compare? I imagine that most llama ranches would do better. But making money is no longer a reason by itself—if ever it was—to own llamas. Llamas for money *and* love!

What if? Spreadsheets as a tool for thinking

A variety of factors will influence your profits. What ratio of male to female babies will be born? What percentage of your adult females will give birth to thriving babies each year? What if prices rise or fall? Are you going to buy adult or juvenile females? Are you going to buy an expensive stud, buy a moderately priced one, or use breeding services? What will your monthly feed and vet bills average? What will be the different financial effects of these choices and outcomes? Pencil and paper will only help a little. Soon you'll be back to "it depends." The questions are just too complex for scratching out a few numbers and saying anything definitive.

Enter the spreadsheet, a tool for thinking. The personal computer revolution of the last decade is based in part upon spreadsheets. People bought computers in order to have the power to analyze various what-ifs. You change some numbers on the computer, which then does dozens, hundreds, or thousands of calculations very quickly. Et voila! You get some more numbers to think about. It was word processing that hooked me on computers, but spreadsheets have kept me up late many times, as I experiment with just one more possibility—and then another.

A spreadsheet is a chart containing words and numbers, arranged in vertical columns and horizontal rows. It can show you things you wouldn't have realized.

Now we'll use spreadsheets on the question, "What's a likely result for an investment in llamas?" The answer that the spreadsheet yields will turn out to be the same answer that observation and anecdotes yielded, "it depends," but at least you'll have two sets of figures to look at. You will have a better sense of the factors that go into "it depends," and it may help in forming your opinion of how llamas compare with other investments.

Assumptions underlying the spreadsheets

Just because the real world is so complex, any spreadsheet forces you to look at what you are assuming, and to simplify the world. It's essential to make a list of your assumptions because writing them down will force you to think about whether they are realistic. Also, when you come back to the spreadsheet later or show it to someone else, the context will be clear. Just as a poorly written paragraph can obscure issues and lead to inaccurate conclusions, so too can a spreadsheet with errors. I hope—but don't guarantee!—that there aren't any errors on these spreadsheets. There may be times when it isn't obvious without a little study how I got certain figures.

I have set up a particular situation, that of an investment of $50,000 buying ten young females and two studs. Then I've run two scenarios. You could run any number of different scenarios.

You could start out with just one stud, but as soon as his daughters are ready to breed, you need a second one. So I made the model simpler by buying them both in the first year. Actually, these two studs are not going to be quite enough for the entire decade. If the first batch of Stud A's daughters are born in Year Three, they will be ready to breed in Year Five. So you breed them to Stud B, and these babies are born in Year Six. This batch are ready to breed in Year Eight—and they are related to both your studs! So by then you need to pay some stud fees or buy an unrelated male. I left this out of the spreadsheet. You might sell one of your studs to buy another, or trade with someone else.

Note that this hypothetical herd is far from the only way to go. If you are planning to breed outstanding llamas that may sell for the top dollar, you may prefer to pay stud fees to outside males or to spend somewhat more for your own stud. You may prefer to buy fewer, more select females.

I completely left out any figures related to the costs of fencing, building sheds, buying pickup trucks, etc. Those expenses would be things you could deduct on a tax return, but they are immensely variable. A more thorough spreadsheet would include them. If you later sell your ranch, improvements to the land may benefit you financially then, in an increased value of the property.

John Schreiber, who is well known for his writings about llamas and finances (see the Resource Guide) has used a figure of around $400 per year per llama for feed and veterinary expenses. That is three or four times higher than many people have said it costs them. I decided to use $200 for all expenses; you'd need to raise it if you carried full mortality insurance. Some walloping veterinary costs could also exceed this amount. There are an assortment of expenses beyond feed and vet bills: equipment; phone bills; advertising; transportation; publications; conferences; and the inevitable miscellany. This figure isn't high enough to cover boarding fees or hiring help.

Another simplifying assumption is that all juvenile llamas are sold in the calendar year in which they were born. In reality, some of them would have been born too late in the year to be weaned and sold till the next year. But it was just easier to figure them this way. The expense figure is calculated on the basis of animals in the herd at year's end, so nothing was allocated for the babies who were sold. This may skew the results somewhat, especially if you encountered major vet expenses with some newborns.

The prices I've chosen may or may not hold true. The $750 for a male llama is high for an average pet or packer; I assumed that if your herd sires had cost you $5000 each, you would end up with males in a variety of price ranges, averaging $750.

These spreadsheets assume that no adult llamas die during the time charted. Inflation could be a consideration in the real world, but not in these spreadsheets.

I decided to sell all the male babies. For the females, I set it up so that in the first scenario all of them are sold. In the second, all males are sold and half of the females would be sold and half kept for breeding. I chose this approach because it seemed to reflect actual practice of many breeders in the 1980s. When the number of babies born would be a fraction, I rounded off. If the figures came out, for example, to 5.6 males and 5.4 females, I rounded off to 6 and 5. (I simply did this in my head rather than with a formula on the spreadsheet.) Since the plan was to sell half the females, a decision had to be made what to do when there was an odd number; in all cases, I sold the extra female.

Now I must admit that spreadsheet thinking is a little like the girl in the old folk tale, going to market fantasizing about how her goose will lay a golden egg and what she will do with the profits. Until you've sold an animal, you haven't really made that profit! This brings to light yet another assumption, which is that you are able to sell all the animals you want to sell at the time you want to; that is, that llamas are totally liquid investments. It's not quite that easy.

As you look at these figures, and compare them with other investments, keep in mind all the hours of hauling hay, waiting for births, training, marketing, shoveling manure, and so forth that go into this business of llamas.

These spreadsheets don't explore the effects of three factors that are very significant: the prices of llamas, the ratio of male to female babies born, and the thriving baby rate. In these scenarios, prices are constant, the births are half and half male and female, and the thriving baby rate is 80%. The thriving baby rate was discussed in previous chapters; it subtracts from 100% the percentage of problem (not pregnant that year) females in a herd and the percentage of reabsorbed fetuses, stillbirths, and babies who die. In reality, all three of these factors are wild cards. You could run spreadsheets showing different possibilities here and you'd get widely varying results. This should keep you from taking any one spreadsheet too seriously.

There is something called "return on investment" that I had on my spreadsheets in the first edition of this book, and I've seen it on spreadsheets other people have created. They didn't seem to be figuring it the same way I was, so when I began working on this revision, I asked my friend Jim Workman, a former lending banker, about it. He said, "ROI is so complex. It seems like everybody has a different way to calculate it." So on his advice, I'm not tackling it. One thing to be aware of is that if you set up a situation where you keep all the llamas or alpacas for a period of years and sell them all at the end, the longer the number of years you keep them, the better your average annual return on investment is going to look—because you've got the cumulative advantage of more babies being born each year.

Let's see what happens with these scenarios.

SCENARIO 1:
SELLING ALL BABIES

Initial investment $50,000.
Steady prices, 50/50 births males/females, thriving baby rate 80%
See the text for other simplifying assumptions.

	YR 1	YR 2	YR 3	YR 4
I. THE HERD--------				
Males, adult	2	2	2	2
Males born AND SOLD	0	0	4	4
Females, adult	0	0	10	10
Females, 1.5 to 2 yrs	0	10	0	0
Females, yearlings	10	0	0	0
Females born, ALL SOLD	0	0	4	4
HERD TOTAL, YEAR END	12	12	12	12
II. PRICES--------				
Male, adult herd sire	$5,000	$5,000	$5,000	$5,000
Male, juvenile	$750	$750	$750	$750
Female, adult, bred	$5,000	$5,000	$5,000	$5,000
Female, juv to 2 yrs	$4,000	$4,000	$4,000	$4,000
III. INCOME--------				
From juvenile males	$0	$0	$3,000	$3,000
From juvenile females	$0	$0	$16,000	$16,000
TOTAL INCOME	$0	$0	$19,000	$19,000
IV. HERD VALUE--------				
Males, adult	$10,000	$10,000	$10,000	$10,000
Females, adult	$0	$0	$50,000	$50,000
Females, 1.5 to 2 yrs	$0	$40,000	$0	$0
Females, yearlings	$40,000	$0	$0	$0
Females juvenile	$0	$0	$0	$0
TOT HERD VALUE, YR END	$50,000	$50,000	$60,000	$60,000
V. EXPENSES @$200/LLAMA	$2,400	$2,400	$2,400	$2,400
TOTAL SPENT TO DATE	**$52,400**	**$54,800**	**$57,200**	**$59,600**
VII. NET INCOME, THIS YR (1)	($2,400)	($2,400)	$16,600	$16,600
VIII. CUMULATIVE INCOME (2)	**($52,400)**	**($54,800)**	**($38,200)**	**($21,600)**
IX. CUM INC + CUR HERD VAL (3)	($2,400)	($4,800)	$21,800	$38,400

NOTES:
(1) TOTAL INCOME MINUS EXPENSES AT $200/LLAMA, FOR CURRENT YEAR
(2) CONSIDERS YOUR ORIGINAL $50,000 AS WELL AS ITEMS IN (1)
   AND IS CUMULATIVE OVER THE YEARS
(3) THE BOTTOM LINE! YOUR CUMULATIVE INCOME PLUS CURRENT HERD VALUE

YR 5	YR 6	YR 7	YR 8	YR 9	YR 10
2	2	2	2	2	2
4	4	4	4	4	4
10	10	10	10	10	10
0	0	0	0	0	0
0	0	0	0	0	0
4	4	4	4	4	4
12	12	12	12	12	12
$5,000	$5,000	$5,000	$5,000	$5,000	$5,000
$750	$750	$750	$750	$750	$750
$5,000	$5,000	$5,000	$5,000	$5,000	$5,000
$4,000	$4,000	$4,000	$4,000	$4,000	$4,000
$3,000	$3,000	$3,000	$3,000	$3,000	$3,000
$16,000	$16,000	$16,000	$16,000	$16,000	$16,000
$19,000	$19,000	$19,000	$19,000	$19,000	$19,000
$10,000	$10,000	$10,000	$10,000	$10,000	$10,000
$50,000	$50,000	$50,000	$50,000	$50,000	$50,000
$0	$0	$0	$0	$0	$0
$0	$0	$0	$0	$0	$0
$0	$0	$0	$0	$0	$0
$60,000	$60,000	$60,000	$60,000	$60,000	$60,000
$2,400	$2,400	$2,400	$2,400	$2,400	$2,400
$62,000	**$64,400**	**$66,800**	**$69,200**	**$71,600**	**$74,000**
$16,600	$16,600	$16,600	$16,600	$16,600	$16,600
($5,000)	**$11,600**	**$28,200**	**$44,800**	**$61,400**	**$78,000**
$55,000	$71,600	$88,200	$104,800	$121,400	$138,000

SCENARIO 2:
BUILDING A HERD & SELLING 1/2 THE FEMALE BABIES

Initial investment $50,000.
Steady prices, 50/50 births males/females, thriving baby rate 80%
See the text for other simplifying assumptions.

	YR 1	YR 2	YR 3	YR 4
I. THE HERD--------				
Males, adult	2	2	2	2
Males born AND SOLD	0	0	4	4
Females, adult	0	0	10	10
Females, 1.5 to 2 yrs	0	10	0	0
Females, yearlings	10	0	0	2
Females born, HALF SOLD	0	0	4	4
HERD TOTAL, YEAR END	12	12	14	16
II. PRICES----------				
Male, adult herd sire	$5,000	$5,000	$5,000	$5,000
Male, juvenile	$750	$750	$750	$750
Female, adult, bred	$5,000	$5,000	$5,000	$5,000
Female, juv to 2 yrs	$4,000	$4,000	$4,000	$4,000
III. INCOME----------				
From juvenile males	$0	$0	$3,000	$3,000
From juvenile females	$0	$0	$8,000	$8,000
TOTAL INCOME	$0	$0	$11,000	$11,000
IV. HERD VALUE--------				
Males, adult	$10,000	$10,000	$10,000	$10,000
Females, adult	$0	$0	$50,000	$50,000
Females, 1.5 to 2 yrs	$0	$40,000	$0	$0
Females, yearlings	$40,000	$0	$0	$8,000
Females, juvenile	$0	$0	$8,000	$8,000
TOT HERD VALUE, YR END	$50,000	$50,000	$68,000	$76,000
V. EXPENSES @$200/LLAMA	$2,400	$2,400	$2,800	$3,200
TOTAL SPENT TO DATE	**$52,400**	**$54,800**	**$57,600**	**$60,800**
VII. NET INCOME, THIS YR (1)	($2,400)	($2,400)	$8,200	$7,800
VIII. CUMULATIVE INCOME (2)	**($52,400)**	**($54,800)**	**($46,600)**	**($38,800)**
IX. CUM INC + CUR HERD VAL (3)	($2,400)	($4,800)	$21,400	$37,200

NOTES:
(1) TOTAL INCOME MINUS EXPENSES AT $200/LLAMA, FOR CURRENT YEAR
(2) CONSIDERS YOUR ORIGINAL $50,000 AS WELL AS ITEMS IN (1)
    AND IS CUMULATIVE OVER THE YEARS
(3) THE BOTTOM LINE! YOUR CUMULATIVE INCOME PLUS CURRENT HERD VALUE

YR 5	YR 6	YR 7	YR 8	YR 9	YR 10
2	2	2	2	2	2
4	5	6	7	7	8
10	12	14	16	18	20
2	2	2	2	2	3
2	2	2	2	3	3
4	5	5	6	7	8
18	20	22	25	28	32
$5,000	$5,000	$5,000	$5,000	$5,000	$5,000
$750	$750	$750	$750	$750	$750
$5,000	$5,000	$5,000	$5,000	$5,000	$5,000
$4,000	$4,000	$4,000	$4,000	$4,000	$4,000
$3,000	$3,750	$4,500	$5,250	$5,250	$6,000
$8,000	$12,000	$12,000	$12,000	$16,000	$16,000
$11,000	$15,750	$16,500	$17,250	$21,250	$22,000
$10,000	$10,000	$10,000	$10,000	$10,000	$10,000
$50,000	$60,000	$70,000	$80,000	$90,000	$100,000
$8,000	$8,000	$8,000	$8,000	$8,000	$12,000
$8,000	$8,000	$8,000	$8,000	$12,000	$12,000
$8,000	$8,000	$8,000	$12,000	$12,000	$16,000
$84,000	$94,000	$104,000	$118,000	$132,000	$150,000
$3,600	$4,000	$4,400	$5,000	$5,600	$6,400
$64,400	**$68,400**	**$72,800**	**$77,800**	**$83,400**	**$89,800**
$7,400	$11,750	$12,100	$12,250	$15,650	$15,600
($31,400)	**($19,650)**	**($7,550)**	**$4,700**	**$20,350**	**$35,950**
$52,600	$74,350	$96,450	$122,700	$152,350	$185,950

Selling all the babies

In both spreadsheets, you begin selling babies in year 3. If you sell them all, the herd size remains static and so does your net income, which works out to $16,600 per year (line VII) before taxes, from year 3 on. In this scenario, the only increase in herd value comes when the young females become adults.

The second line in section V, "Total Investment to Date," shows what you've spent for everything; Line VIII shows your cumulative income over the ten years. For the first five years, you're recouping the amount that you spent, and for the second five you've making money. At the end of ten years, you've earned back all that you spent and $78,000 more—and since you have a herd worth $60,000, line IX shows the figure of $138,000, the sum of cumulative income and current herd value.

Building a herd

In this scenario, you begin with the same herd but you keep half the female babies that are born and add them to the herd, so that by the end of the ten years, you have a herd of 32. I was surprised to see that it this picture, your cumulative income doesn't come out of the red until the eighth year! This is largely because of the high expenses, in this model, of keeping the young females from birth until they produce. At the end of ten years, you would have $35,950 more in cash than you had spent up till then. Your major profits would be in your herd, which would have a value of $150,000.

So these spreadsheets indicate that you can make money on llamas, but that these scenarios at least are not wildly lucrative. Remembering the rule of 72, If you invested money at 6% per year, at the end of twelve years, you would have doubled your money. Both of these scenarios do considerably more than that, in ten years.

What about taxes?

You always have to think about taxes in considering any investment. Depreciation, llama losses sheltering other income, depreciation recapture if you sell a purchased animal, regular income tax, self-employment tax, state income and/or sales taxes—all these factors have their ups and downs on your income.

One nice thing about buying llamas is that you can depreciate their cost over several years. This will nicely shelter quite a lot of other income. Of course, if you ever sell those animals, the shoe will be on the other foot.

You may hear that you need to have a certain number of llamas for the IRS to consider that llama breeding is a business for you rather than a hobby. I've heard breeders—and accountants, I think—say this, but other breeders and my accountant have said it's not the case. So I leave it up to you to form your own conclusions. I haven't heard this theory as much in recent years.

You do need to conduct yourself in a business-like manner, keep records, show a profit motive, and so forth. It's recommended to make a profit some years!

A more enjoyable tax effect of llama breeding is that no tax is due until you have a profit. So if good old Millie produces seven daughters in a row, and if you keep them, those lovely ladies haven't been taxed yet. If you have a savings account, the only way to avoid tax on savings is to plunk as much of it as you can into an IRA or similar plan—and then you can't get to it without penalty. Your llama herd can keep on increasing in number and thus value until you decide to sell some. In effect, you're using pre-tax dollars—or pre-tax llamas—to build your herd. Real estate offers a similar benefit—if it increases in value—in that no tax is due until it's sold. This benefit doesn't show up in the two spreadsheets in this chapter, but it would weigh in favor of building up the herd.

Also, once you have a herd of llamas, comparing them to other investments involves thinking about taxes. If you sell, you'll have a lot less money to put into something else after you pay taxes on your profits.

Doing your own spreadsheets

If you have access to a computer and a spreadsheet program, you may find it very helpful in clarifying your thinking to make your own assumptions and set up your own spreadsheets. Here are some details of how I set these up.

In Section I, The Herd, I put the number of adult males in for the first year, and then had each subsequent year equal to the one before it. For the females, the adult females of any year equal the adult females plus the 1.5 to 2 year olds from the prior year. The 1.5

to 2 group of the year are last year's yearlings; and the yearlings of the year are the females born minus the females sold in the prior year. All of this can be set up with formulas and then the formulas can be copied from one year all the way across the page. So I set up a template form, and then saved the file under different names once it's been filled in with the scenarios.

For the numbers of animals born, it could have been set up with formulas, but since I didn't want to work with, say, 4.7 females, I simply did my own rounding off. Also, I wasn't sure how to tell the program that if an odd number of babies were born, the extra one should be male. So I just plugged those numbers in. Because I did it this way, two of my three variables—male/female ratio and thriving baby rate—are a little more variable than the formula.

For the total investment to date, I began with $50,000 then added year one's expenses @ $200/llama.

If you don't have a computer, you can of course do something of this sort with calculator and paper. But it's more fun on a computer! However you do it, it's good to take a break from crunching numbers now and then, and think about the living creatures behind them. That's the point of the exercise, after all.

CHAPTER ELEVEN

Llamas in the Future

"AS LONG AS LOVE and fascination for llamas remain the top priority, the industry will thrive," Beula Williams said. "The profit to be gained from llamas is not money alone, but rather the total experience of being a shepherd—from the challenge of breeding to the miracle of birth and renewal of life."

Beula and her husband Jim were the first llama breeders I ever met. For this chapter, I asked them and several other long-time llama breeders about their vision of llamas in the future.

It turned out to be an enjoyable question to ask, because everyone expressed such love for llamas. Their dreams and ideas for the future grow out of the great delight they take in llamas. Llamas for love far outweighed llamas for money in everyone's comments. It was a pleasure to hear this over and over from industry leaders.

Kay Patterson, who's been at the heart of the growth in llama popularity, said, "My vision? That people would always keep foremost in their minds that llamas are fun! Each of us is responsible to give something back to these wonderful animals who have blessed our lives in so many ways. We can give back to them through our time, in money for research, and in other ways.

"Llamas teach us patience and love, and those are the two most important things in life for me."

Nancy Calhoun, one of the first Eastern breeders, said, "My enthusiasm was at a very high level when we began in 1977, and it has only continued to climb. I'd like to see more llamas going into nursing homes, schools, and parades, and on the trail. The future is extraordinarily bright for llamas, no question!"

Susan Torrey has greatly enjoyed her many years with llamas. "They are unique among companion animals. It's like owning a 400 pound vegetarian cat. People who ask what they're good for may not be satisfied with the quantity of things we can tell them about llama uses, because the real answer is qualitative. Raising and working with llamas brings us back to ourselves and to nature.

"Gaining their trust, watching them birth, learning to care for a large animal, enjoying their beauty—these are really empowering experiences. They're peaceable, high-touch experiences that help balance our increasingly stress-prone existence. Add to this the fact that llamas are smaller, easier to care for, and less intimidating than traditional livestock, and the llama industry should remain lively for a long time to come."

Jamie Sharp, one of the founders of LANA, said, "Llamas are willing to interact, species-to-species. You can have a unique friendship with a llama because of its intelligence and its willingness to trust you."

Stephen Biggs, a past president of ILA, was one of the first people to do llama packing commercially. He reflected, "I see people in the mountains exquisitely enjoying themselves. They come out of busy, stressful lives, and get in touch with parts of themselves that have been ignored for who knows how long. There's a transformation that takes place in proximity to the beauty and serenity of the llamas." He sees a good future for llama packing.

Steve Rolfing, also a commercial packer and another past president of ILA, is enthusiastic about packing too. "The low impact of llamas will make their use spread. Hunters will use them more. Forest Service trail crews are already using them in California and Colorado, and that will spread to other parts of the country."

"On a world wide scale, I see the popularity of llamas increasing in Europe, especially northern Europe. Besides North America, there are already beginnings in New Zealand and Australia. I think the South Americans are going to become more selective about their breeding."

Coral Gibson, a Canadian who has served on the ILA Board of Directors, said, "I really hope that the llama community maintains the spirit of camaraderie and mutual respect which it has now. I would like our level of professionalism to continue to increase, and I would like llamas to be taken seriously as a permanent part of the livestock

business, by governments and other livestock associations in both Canada and the U.S."

Coral feels these changes are underway. "We are growing up. People are looking for answers that we won't have until we commit to much more research. We don't realize from one ILA conference to the next how much we've evolved in that year."

Trainer Bobra Goldsmith said, "I'm very interested in driving as part of the future of llamas in this country, because I think some of llamas' appeal is their versatility. There certainly is a question right now in some people's minds as to whether llamas will ever be good driving animals. I say we won't know till we try, and I have a good deal of faith that they will be."

One of the things that excites me most about llamas in the future is the deepening of communication between llamas and people. I see the interactions becoming ever more subtle and interesting, from the evolution of training methods to vaster realms. Penelope Smith, who communicates telepathically with animals, now owns two geldings (one from my herd!) with whom she and her husband, Michel Sherman, hike frequently. She has spoken at llama gatherings on this topic, and received a tremendous amount of interest.

Many people speak of a spiritual aspect to llamas. As Steve Rolfing put it, "There's an enduring attraction to llamas—they have a mystical appeal, or whatever you want to call it. You know that look in their eyes when you sit out in the pasture with them? Most people feel it right away."

As time goes on in this fast-paced, surprising, and often difficult world we live in, llamas and their owners are going to be contributing to society in a spectrum of wonderful ways. If your heart leads you to llamas, do come into the field.

CHAPTER TWELVE

Resource Guide

WANT TO know more about llamas? This chapter lists a selection of the llama and alpaca resources available, with ordering information. To find out about new publications, watch for ads (particularly classifieds) and reviews in the magazines. This list doesn't include children's material or out-of-print items.

Because the North American llama and alpaca industries are so new, there is still much to learn. Many people have shared their ideas and observations, often through self-publishing. Bear in mind that some of the information in the publications listed below may have already become outdated, and that some things presented as fact may be vigorously disputed by other llama fanciers.

Phone numbers are included when the vendors are known to accept phone orders, usually with a credit card. Please add sales tax if you order within the state where you live.

A slightly different version of this list is published by the International Llama Association, and is included with their free llama catalog.

Books and booklets

Alpacas: the World's Finest Livestock Investment. Enthusiastic, informative 26-page booklet available from AOBA, listed under organizations.

Barkman, Betty and Paul, *A Well-Trained Llama.* 34190 Lodge Road, Tollhouse, CA 93667. $20 postpaid. Revised edition, many photos. By a pair who have trained everything from elephants to reptiles, with much llama experience.

Bodington, Helen, *Llama Training on Your Own: Step by Step Instructions*. Polite Pets, 697 Fawn Drive, San Anselmo, CA 94960. 1986. $20 postpaid. Two lessons a day for five days, one lesson a day for the next four, and suggestions for further practice.

Burt, Sandi, *Llamas: An Introduction to Care, Training, and Handling*. Alpine Publications. $21.45 postpaid from LLasa LLama Ranch and Farm Supply, 11383 Yuba Ridge Drive, Nevada City, CA 95959. (800) 230-5262. 190-page introduction to llamas, with photos, graphs, lists. Chapters cover acquisition, care, housing, feed, shelter, grooming, exhibiting, breeding, health care.

Calle Escobar, Rigoberto, *Animal Breeding and Production of American Camelids*. Lima, Peru, 1984. Available from Llamas Magazine Store, address/phone listed below. $34.70 postpaid. 358 pages with charts, sketches and photos. Translated from Spanish. In three parts: General Information about Camelids, Alpaca Management, and Alpaca Improvement and Productivity.

Daugherty, Stanlynn, *Packing with Llamas*. Juniper Ridge Press, PO Box 1278, Olympia, WA 98507. (800) 869-7342. Third edition, 1994. $13.95 postpaid. 210 pages, 75 photos. A comprehensive introduction to llama packing, covering selection and care of llamas, training for the trail, equipment, on the trail, etc. Includes pack bag pattern and backcountry recipes.

Faiks-Lyons, Jan, Jim Faiks, and Phyllis Tozier, *Llama Training: Who's in Charge?* Faiks' Alpacas and Llamas, Box 521152, Big Lake, AK 99652. Second edition, 1985. $15.00 postpaid. The first llama training manual published. Incudes a discussion of the training methods used with a 'berserk' male.

Fowler, Murray E., DVM, *Medicine and Surgery of South American Camelids: Llama, Alpaca, Vicuna, Guanaco*. Iowa State Univ. Press, 2121 S. State Ave, Ames, IA 50010. (515) 292-0140. 1989. $76.95 postpaid. This 400-page textbook and reference for veterinarians will be of interest to many llama breeders as well. Written by one of the best-known llama veterinary researchers. With over 400 photos, plus drawings and tables. Health care, disease treatment, surgical procedures, anatomy, physiology.

Franklin, Dr. William L., and Kelly J. Powell, *Guard Llamas*. Iowa State University, Extension Distribution Center, 119 Printing and Publications Bldg, Ames, IA 50011. Call (515) 294-5247 for ordering details. Informative 12-page booklet.

Freeman, Myra, *Heat Stress: Prevention, Management and Treatment in Llamas*. Southern States Llama Association, 1315 Bell's Hollow, Blairsville, GA 30512. $10 postpaid. A short compilation of techniques from the hot Southeast.

Harmon, David, and Amy S. Rubin, *Llamas on the Trail, A Packer's Guide*, 1993. Mountain Press Publishing Company, PO Box 2399, Missoula, MT 59806. $15.00. Two experienced llama packers and writers discuss llama packing, with photos.

Hart, Rosana, *Living with Llamas: Tales from Juniper Ridge*. Juniper Ridge Press, Box 1278, Olympia, WA 98507-1278. (800) 869-7342. Third edition, 1987. $13.95 postpaid. 192 pages. A personal account of Kelly's and my llama adventures, with photos and information woven into the story.

Hoffman, Clare, DVM, and Ingrid Asmus, *Caring for Llamas: A Health and Management Guide*. Rocky Mountain Llama and Alpaca Association, 168 Emerald Mtn. Ct., Livermore, CO 80536. Revised edition, 1993. $20.95 postpaid. 150 pages. The most comprehensive manual of llama care available. Basic care and management, diseases and treatments, first aid. Troubleshooting charts for identifying emergencies. Illustrations. Extremely useful!

International Llama Association, PO Box 37505, Denver, CO 80237. (303) 756-9004. ILA Educational Brochures: #3, *Llama Facts for New Owners*; #4, *Llama Medical Management*; #5, *Llama Housing and Fencing*; #6, *Feeding Llamas*; #7, *Llama Herd Management*; #8, *So You Want to Be a Llama Mama! Notes on Reproduction, Birthing and Care of the Newborn Llama*; #9, *Llama Wool*, #10, *Packing with Llamas*. 50 cents each. Short, packed with information, written by authorities on the topics. Reference Brochure *Books, Videotapes, and Magazines about Llamas and Alpacas*, free.

Johnson, LaRue W., DVM, PhD, Guest Editor, *Veterinary Clinics of North America: Food Animal Practice (Llama Medicine)*. W.B. Saunders Co., PO Box 6467, Duluth, MN 55806-9854. (800) 654-2452. Vol 5, No. 1, March 1989. $29 postpaid. 236 pages. Includes articles by over a dozen contributors, mostly veterinarians and professors, on llama medicine. Useful for veterinarians and llama owners. Also available in Spanish.

Jones-Ley, Susan, *Llamas: Woolly, Winsome, and Wonderful*. Photography by Susan, PO Box 1038, Dublin, OH 43017. $12.95

postpaid. 68 pages. Text with 73 photos, 33 in color, from many llama farms, by the best-known llama photographer.

Markham, Doyle. *Llamas are the Ultimate.* Snake River Llamas, 1480 Antares Dr., Idaho Falls, ID 83402. $16.95 postpaid. 1990.Training, feeding, packing, hunting, fishing, and care.

McGee, Marty, with Linda Tellington-Jones, *Llama Handling and Training, the TTEAM Approach,* 1992. Zephyr Farm Press, 4251 Pulver Rd, Dundee, NY 14837. (607) 243-5282 $28.25 postpaid. Comprehensive (over 200 page) manual on TTEAM methods for llamas, with case histories, photos, diagrams.

Morris, Joy, DVM, and Myra Freeman, *Llama First Aid for the Barn.* Southern States Llama Association, 1315 Bell's Hollow, Blairsville, GA 30512. $7 postpaid. 26 pages.

Pryor, Karen, *Don't Shoot the Dog! The New Art of Teaching and Training.* Bantam, 1985. Although there's not a word about llamas in here, this is my favorite llama training book, as the principles apply to all animals, including people. The author is a noted dolphin trainer, who has worked with llamas more recently.

Schreiber, John, *Today and Tomorrow Llama Investment Analysis.* Schreiber's Stoney Brook Farm, W338 S9025 Highway E, Mukwonago, WI 53149. Revised edition, 1990. $21.95 postpaid. Numerical analysis of supply and demand, with spreadsheet-type projections of potential returns, by a llama breeder who works in the investment field.

Umbach, Cutler. *Llama Herd Health Management in West Central Idaho.* High Llama, PO Box 172-LLM, McCall, ID 83638. 1989. $5 postpaid. 24 pages. Synopsis of practices at their ranch. Also available: free booklet, "Tips to the New Llama Buyer."

Videotapes

(All tapes are available in VHS, and some are in Beta. Foreign formats are not generally available, but ask.)

Basic TTEAM with Llamas, Featuring Marty McGee. Juniper Ridge Press, Box 1278, Olympia, WA 98507-1278. (800) 869-7342. $67 postpaid. Two hours. Application to llamas of useful and unique techniques originally developed with horses.

Breeding, Birthing, and Newborn Care. Tape 2 of the series, *All about Llamas with Paul and Sally Taylor.* Taylor/Gavin

Communications, Box 4323, Bozeman, MT 59772. (406) 586-6872. $41.95 postpaid. 60-minutes, with handbook. This videotape shows the normal breeding and birthing processes with many llamas.

Fences, Barns, and Feeders. Betty Barkman, 34190 Lodge Rd, Tollhouse, CA 93667. (209) 855-6227; Visa, MC orders to (800) 232-7630. $43.45 postpaid. Many useful ideas from a variety of ranches. Also covers gates, shelters, safety tips, and more.

In Search of the Ideal Llama. Saltspring Island Llamas and Alpacas, 291 Long Harbour Rd, RR3, C-16, Ganges, BC, Canada V0S 1E0. Phone/fax (604) 537-9446. $63.45(US) postpaid. Produced and written by Richard and Maggie Krieger, with well-known llama veterinarian Dr. Murray Fowler. Analysis of llama conformation, including how to detect the less obvious anomalies.

Five Star Llama Packing. Juniper Ridge Press, P O Box 1278, Olympia, WA 98507-1278. (800) 869-7342. $41.95 postpaid. Two hours, produced by Kelly Hart. Experienced commercial llama packers Stephen Biggs, Stanlynn Daugherty, Bobra Goldsmith, Francie Greth-Peto, and Tom Landis discuss and demonstrate all aspects of llama packing. Several pack trips are shown.

Let's Go Packing, Tape #3 of the series, *All about Llamas with Paul and Sally Taylor.* Taylor/Gavin Communications, Box 4323, Bozeman, MT 59772. (406) 586-6872. 1989. $41.95 postpaid. Fifty minutes. Includes basic training, conditioning, equipment, fighting teeth removal, toenail trimming, and a Montana pack trip, by experienced commercial llama packers Renee and Will Gavin.

Llama Basics, Tape #1 of the series, *All about Llamas with Paul and Sally Taylor.* Taylor/Gavin Communications, Box 4323, Bozeman, MT 59772. (406) 586-6872. $41.95 postpaid. 40 minutes. Introduction to llamas: nutrition, fencing, facilities, evolution, and behavior, shot at the Taylor's beautiful ranch in Montana.

Llama Reproduction: A Neonatal Clinic with LaRue W. Johnson, DVM, PhD. Juniper Ridge Press, PO Box 1278, Olympia, WA 98507-1278, (800) 869-7342. 1989. $97 postpaid. Lectures, slides, videotape of an actual hands-on clinic with a well-known llama researcher. Demonstrates a variety of different birth presentations and how to deliver them, using plastic uteruses and stillborn crias. 3 1/2 hours, set of two tapes and one booklet.

Llama Training with Bobra Goldsmith: What Every Llama Should Know. Two hours. Juniper Ridge Press, Box 1278, Olympia,

WA 98507-1278. (800) 869-7342. $67 postpaid. Two hours, produced by Kelly Hart. A foremost llama trainer shows her methods. Covers initial contact, the slow motion technique of haltering, leading with a light hand, loading in vehicles, kushing, some difficult llamas, developing trust and willingness.

Llama Trekkers, Betty Barkman, 34190 Lodge Rd, Tollhouse, CA 93667. (209) 855-6227; Visa, MC orders to (800) 232-7630. $43.45 postpaid. A training experience for those ready to train their first packers.

Step by Step Shearing for Alpacas and Llamas, 65 mins, $53.50 postpaid from Main Street Video, 2602 Westridge Ave W., Suite P102, Tacoma, WA 98466. (800) 275-8566. With Ted and Elaine Chepolis; covers preparatory grooming, the tools, restraining methods, fleece preparation, storage, marketing.

Training Llamas to Drive, With Bobra Goldsmith. Juniper Ridge Press, PO Box 1278, Olympia, WA 98507. (800) 869-7342. 1989. $67 ppd. 2 hours. Preparations, fitting the harness, ground driving, introducing the llama to the cart, and riding in the cart.

The TTEAM Approach to Llama Herd Management. Zephyr Farm Press, 4251 Pulver Rd, Dundee, NY 14837. (607) 243-5282. $33.95 postpaid. 45 minute program keyed to the TTEAM book (listed under McGee in the books section). Focusses on starting young llamas and herd management chores.

Why Llamas? Juniper Ridge Press, Box 1278, Olympia, WA 98507. (800) 869-7342. $31.95 postage paid.   Fifty minute video introducing llamas, produced by Kelly Hart. Llamas doing everything from giving birth to taking part in obstacle races; interviews with llama owners.

Periodicals

Alpacas, PO Box 1968, Manhattan, KS 66502. Quarterly supplement to *Llama Banner*, listed below.

The Backcountry Llama, Noel McRae, Editor, 2857 Rose Valley Loop, Kelso, WA 98626. $8.00 per year. A small newsletter about packing with llamas, published six times per year.

Canadian Llama News, Margaret Brewster and Marie Lammle, Editors, 6012 - Third St., S.W., Calgary, Alberta, Canada T2H 0H9, $20 per year. (That's $20 Canadian in Canada, $20 US everywhere else.) Bi-monthly.

Llama Banner, PO Box 1968, Manhattan, KS 66502. (913) 537-0320. Bimonthly, $24 per year. Describing itself as "the promotional tool of the llama industry," this glossy magazine has lots of ads as well as articles, news of shows, etc. I enjoy many of the interesting first-person articles by llama owners.

Llama Life, 2259 County Road 220, Durango, CO 81301. (303) 259-0002. Edited by Terry Price. Published quarterly. $16/year. Glossy black and white quarterly newspaper. News, photos, ads, feature articles by a variety of llama owners, indepth coverage of markets and auctions. Has won awards from industry associations. I appreciate editor Terry Price's willingness to tell it like he sees it and to encourage others to do the same; in these pages you will find the liveliest arguments and discussions in print on llamas.

The Llama Link. Drawer 1995, Kalispell, MT 59903. (406) 752-2569. Edited by Jan and Dar Wassink. A free monthly classified and display ad publication, with some feature writing.

Llamas Magazine, PO Box 100, Herald, CA 95638. (209) 223-0469. (See also its Store, listed on next page.) Edited by Cheryl Dal Porto. Published eight times a year. Subscription $25. From Canada, $30 US. Other foreign, $35. This award-winning magazine (often called "the magazine" in llama circles) includes articles, questions and answers, letters, reviews, and ads. Many color photos. If you are going to subscribe to just one magazine, make it *Llamas*.

Organizations

Alpaca Owners and Breeders Association (AOBA), c/o Hobart Office Services, Ltd. PO Box 1992, Estes Park, CO 80517-1992. Conferences, directory, subscription to *Alpacas*, publications.

Alpaca and Llama Show Association (ALSA), 5505 Dutch Lane, Johnstown, OH 43031. (614) 967-6636. Publishes an annual magazine distributed free at shows. This group sponsors shows and trains judges. The *ALSA Handbook* is available for $20, and covers show guidelines, class descriptions, judging criteria, and association bylaws. $35 membership includes the handbook.

Canadian Llama Association. PO Box 476, Bragg Creek, Alberta, Canada T0L 0K0. (403) 949-2955.

International Lama Registry, Box 7166, Rochester, MN, 55903. (507) 281-2178. For both llamas and alpacas.

International Llama Association (ILA), PO Box 370505, Denver, CO 80237. (303) 756-9004; fax: (303) 756-8794. For information, call their toll-free number, (800) WHY-LAMA. Bimonthly newsletter and other publications, annual conference, promotion, membership directory, etc. The largest llama association, with numerous active chapters, ILA publishes the annual and free *Llama Catalog: A Directory of Llama Products and Services*, which lists breeders and suppliers of all kinds of things. (People pay to be listed in this; being listed is not an ILA endorsement.)

Llama Association of North America (LANA), PO Box 1882, Minden, NV 89423. Annual expo and llama show, quarterly newsletter, directory, etc. Especially active on the west coast.

Rocky Mountain Lama Association (RMLA), 593 19 3/4 Rd, Grand Junction, CO 81503. RMLA now draws members from all over. This is in part because of the emphasis on doing things with llamas that characterizes this group. Annual conference, membership directory, bi-monthly newsletter. One popular feature of this organization is the by-mail lending library of books, videos, and articles.

Llama and alpaca supplies

Here are the names of a few llama supply businesses. For more, see the ads in the llama magazines (especially *Llamas*) or attend a conference (especially ILA).

Llamas Magazine Store, PO Box 100, Herald, CA 95638 or 44 Main Street, Jackson, CA 95642. Many of the items listed here may be ordered from this store, which also carries gift items; its phone/fax is (209) 223-5529.

LLasa LLama Ranch and Farm Supply, 11383 Yuba Ridge Drive, Nevada City, CA 95959. (800) 230-LAMA.

Quality Llama Products, 6615 SW McVey, Redmond, OR 97756. (800) 638-4689. Gift items, tack, publications.etc. Formerly known as Llamas and More.

Rocky Mountain Llamas, 7202 N 45th St, Longmont, CO 80503. (303) 530-5575. Particularly for the equipment designed by Bobra Goldsmith, but they carry a variety of other items as well.

Index

Photo credits

Carroll Albert, Albert's Llamasery: 31, 56, 57, 70
Heather Bamford, East Fork Ranch: Back cover, 71, 161
Steve Johnson: Frontispiece, 24, 89
All other photos by Rosana or Kelly Hart.

Also from Juniper Ridge Press

BOOKS

Living with Llamas: Tales from Juniper Ridge, by Rosana Hart. Writing with warmth and humor, Rosana tells the story of her life with a herd of llamas. People write to us that they can't put the book down. Over fifty photos, including a birth sequence. 192 pages, $11.95 plus shipping.

Packing with Llamas. Author Stanlynn Daugherty draws on her expertise as a commercial llama packer to describe every aspect of llama packing. Over 75 photographs inform and inspire. 210 pages, $11.95 plus shipping.

VIDEOTAPES

Basic T.T.E.A.M. with Llamas, Featuring Marty McGee. A well-known horse training method, here applied successfully to llamas. $65 + shipping.

Five Star Llama Packing. This entertaining program is loaded with llama-packing information, opinions, and demonstrations. $39.95+shpg.

Llama Reproduction: A Neonatal Clinic with LaRue W.Johnson, DVM, PhD. Covers breeding, birth, and newborn care. $95 + shipping.

Llama Training with Bobra Goldsmith: What Every Llama Should Know. An excellent way to get to know llamas better, featuring a noted llama trainer. $65 + shipping.

Telepathic Communication with Animals, Featuring Penelope Smith In this fascinating program, Penelope Smith demonstrates how she communicates telepathically with animals. Not a step-by-step how-to, but you can learn a lot. $29.95 + shipping.

Training Llamas to Drive, with Bobra Goldsmith. Introducing this enjoyable activity. $65 + shipping.

Why Llamas? If you've ever wondered, "Why llamas?" you will wonder no more after seeing this delightful videotape. $29.95 + shipping.

ORDER FORM

TO: Juniper Ridge Press, PO Box 1278, Olympia, WA 98507. (800) 869-7342 or (206) 705-1328

Please send me:

BOOKS

____ *Living with Llamas: Tales from Juniper Ridge*, by Rosana Hart. 1991. $11.95 postpaid.

____ *Llamas for Love and Money*, (this book), by Rosana Hart. 1994. $16.95 postpaid.

____ *Packing with Llamas*, by Stanlynn Daugherty, 1994. $13.95 postpaid.

VIDEOTAPES

____ *Basic T. T.E.A.M. with Llamas.* Two hours, VHS. $67.00 postpaid.

____ *Five Star Llama Packing.* VHS, 2 hours, $41.95 postpaid.

____ *Llama Reproduction: A Neonatal Clinic with LaRue W. Johnson, DVM, PhD.* VHS, 3 1/2 hours, two tapes + booklet, $97 postpaid.

____ *Llama Training with Bobra Goldsmith: What Every Llama Should Know.* Two hours, VHS, $67.00 postpaid.

____ *Telepathic Communication with Animals, Featuring Penelope Smith.* VHS, 46 minutes. $31.95.

____ *Why Llamas?* Fifty minutes, VHS, $31.95 postpaid.

____ I'm enclosing an additional $1.50 for you to send my order by first class mail. (The prices above include fourth class mail.)

____ Please send me your free descriptive catalog.

Total enclosed:

Check, money order, MasterCard, and Visa welcomed. Make checks (US funds) out to Juniper Ridge Press. Call Juniper Ridge Press toll-free at (800) 869-7342, from the US and Canada, for faster credit card orders or for information. Call us if you're interested in quantity discounts.

If you are paying with a credit card, is it MC? ____ or Visa? ____
Card number:
Expiration date:
Signature and phone number:

PLEASE PRINT LEGIBLY

NAME:
ADDRESS:
CITY, STATE, ZIP: